Battles of a Bipolar Buddhist

Kitty Richards

Battles of a Bipolar Buddhist / Kitty Richards

ISBN-13: 9781490932613 (paperback)
ASIN: BOOCUPG6BU (e-book)

1.Memoir 2.Creative non-fiction

You may contact the author via email at:
kittyk1963@gmail.com

Forward to the third edition

Due to the many changes in my life and
perspective since the original publication of this
memoir in 2013, some changes to this book
became necessary. Hence the second and third
editions. I offer my sincere gratitude to all those
who responded so positively and constructively to
the previous editions. Their insights helped mo-
tivate me to dig deeper to more clearly convey the
truth of my life.

A Note from the Author

Dear Reader,

Thanks to some tremendous good fortune, a woman I hardly knew encouraged me to overcome my fears and doubts and write this memoir. And, if that wasn't enough, then the book actually won a contest! I'm so grateful for this. Now, you have elected to start reading it, and I can't thank *you* enough for taking the time to consider my story.

Former American First Lady Eleanor Roosevelt, who had a major role in drafting the Universal Declaration of Human Rights, wrote, "It is my conviction that there is almost no arena of life which we cannot transform according to our own desires if we want something badly enough, if we have faith in it, and if we work for it with all our hearts.... One thing I believe profoundly: We make our own history. The course of history grows out of the ideas, the beliefs, the values, the dreams of the people."[1]

Many famous historical and heroic figures have experienced altered states of consciousness, also referred to as neurobiological disorders, mental disorders, emotional disorders, post traumatic stress disorder (PTSD), chemical imbalances in the brain, nervous system dysfunction, brain disorders, mental illness, mental health challenges, dangerous gifts, and so on. There is much speculation about the causes of these experiences, whether they are from family and/or societal dysfunction, traumas, genetics, something else or none of the above. While some people seem to have all of the above-mentioned issues in their histories, disorders like mine hit others due to a single stressor or for no obvious reason at all. Hopefully more research will increase our understanding.

As to those who have gone before us, I greatly admire the well-known as well as the many unknown people of history who dealt with these difficulties and achieved great things. But it is my fervent hope that this book about the extraordinary events in the life of an ordinary person like me will combat stigma and discrimination, promote kindness towards ourselves and others, and increase dialogue about these issues plaguing our society, about the condition of our current mental health system, and about the precious potential to be nurtured within all people, including the extremely artistic temperament.

Lastly, although all the people in this book are real, some names have been changed to protect folks' privacy.

Warm regards,

Kitty

Battles
of a
Bipolar
Buddhist

CHAPTER ONE

The story of my birth was a well-kept family secret. An autobiographical piece I once published struck my favorite aunt with the karmic relevance of my own beginnings. It was then she shared this secret with me. But long before I left childhood, I was already convinced that the day I was born in 1963 was the unluckiest day in the history of the world and I the world's unluckiest soul.

My stepmother entered the bedroom I shared with five other girls. That same sour-faced frown I'd lived with for seven years changed to a sheepish grin as our eyes met.

She must've just gotten her hair done, I thought. The black curls tightly hugged her white scalp. Not one strand was gray now.

"Hi, Kathy."

"Hi, Margaret."

"It's been a while."

"Nine months to be exact."

"I'm sorry you didn't get to come home for Christmas."

"That's all right. I didn't mind. I got to spend it with two girls my age from the Bahamas who couldn't get home then either," I said. But I thought, *It did kind of hurt actually, since you and Dad could've easily driven the hour and a half to come get me.* "And our housemother took good care of us."

Our boarding school housemother, Mrs. Kind, reminded me a lot of Margaret's mother. Plump, with a twinkle in her eye and a ready laugh, Grandma had loved to march my three siblings and me into the wilds of the land she and Grandpa owned next door to us. With a rifle on her shoulder to scare off rogue motorcyclists if they were back there trespassing, she led us single file, passed the ruins of some old cement buildings where Dad dumped our garbage. We explored some underground tunnels together, but the use of those tunnels and broken down buildings always remained a mystery to me.

Mrs. Kind didn't carry a rifle, and she hadn't sat me on her lap when I was little to read me a Bible story like Grandma once had, but she was a big comfort away from home.

I motioned for Margaret to have a seat on my bunk. I took the one next to her.

"Well, Kathy, I wanted to come and see you to tell you how sorry I am. I did some really rotten things to you up in Caledonia, and I feel really bad about it. Ever since we moved down to Florida, I've been going to this new church in Orlando, and Kathy, I've been Born Again. Ever since then, I've been thinking about how badly I treated you all those years. It wasn't right. You didn't deserve that. I'm so sorry. I had to come and tell you. To ask you to forgive me."

She said all this with tears in her swollen, bloodshot eyes. There was no doubt in my mind she was sincere. But I was not moved. I didn't feel anything from her apology. Surprise, yes. It shocked me to see her like this. The woman who'd always called my name like it was a swear word.

But now, it was my turn. She'd left herself

wide open. Was she gonna get an earful!

Well, Margaret, since we're being so honest and all, I'd like to ask you some questions. Why did you sit with Patty on her bed having long, intimate conversations all those years while I could only pass by her room wishing it were me in there with you? When I helped you fold the laundry, why didn't you at least talk with me around the laundry basket? You bossed me, paddled me, and even called me a bitch so many times I lost count. Do you know I left that house of yours feeling like a second-class citizen? You told Brian and me that children were to be seen and not heard, especially at the dinner table, but then your precious Patty was allowed to monopolize the dinner conversation every night!

I dreaded coming home from school every afternoon. And if I didn't see your blue station wagon when I came in the back door of the garage, I dreaded the sound of the garage door going up.

Oh, and what about Gary? Just like you, your son couldn't stand me. And when he and I argued over a bike, he assaulted me and got away with it. You never even punished him. But he was a year older and bigger than me! Then without any explanation you banned me from playing with him and his friends anymore, which I'd been doing for years. How was any of that fair?

Worst of all was when you forbid me from walking around on Grandma and Grandpa's land. For years, I'd never gotten hurt back there. It was my favorite place where I felt safe to be myself. Playing in the barn, eating wild cherries, finding secret places. I liked being alone out there. But then you told me it was too dangerous and still you shooed me out the door to 'go play' in the yard. There weren't even trees in the yard! Nothing but grass. How was that going to be any fun?

You ignored me so well you didn't even know what was happening in my bedroom for years—right under your nose!

I would've screamed all of this at her at an octave loud enough to break crystal if I'd thought of it. But I didn't. None of this even entered my mind until much later in life. It didn't occur to me to pummel her when she was down. And I didn't exactly know how to communicate these thoughts and feelings anyway. No one had ever shown me how.

So many times living in Margaret's house, when I became taller than her five-foot frame, I wanted to punch her lights out when she'd yell at me in front of my father during an argument between us. I figured I probably would've won a fistfight with her too. But, of course, I never tried. She was an adult. She had the upper hand. She always had my father silently standing on her side. And, of course, I didn't want to punch her now. She looked too pathetic.

"It's okay, Margaret. I forgive you."

And that was it. Her conscience was clear, her guilt purged. She could leave with a light and happy heart.

It's all better now, huh, Margaret? For you maybe. It was gonna take me decades to even realize I needed to heal from her and all the trauma in that bedroom.

Unbeknownst to me, Dad had already decided to leave her. Had she thought her apology would somehow save their marriage?

Dad came to pick me up for the summer break the day after Margaret's visit. His thinning hair had not yet begun to turn grey. His steel-blue eyes always seemed to stare at me rather than invite me in. After not seeing him for nine months I got a split-second obligatory hug. He yanked his arms away so fast I felt like an anathema.

"I'm divorcing your stepmother, Kathy."

"Oh?" I said.

He seemed compelled to explain. "Margaret's ultimatum was the last straw. I should have never given in to her demands. She said it was either you or her when we moved to Florida, and I really wanted to give our marriage one more try. But sending you to boarding school didn't make any difference. I've fallen out of love with her."

I didn't know what to say, so I asked him if he'd like to go for a walk around the campus. I showed him my horse at the stables—Big Red. Dad may have thought he did me wrong by sending me away. (In fact, years later Dad would shed his own tears of regret. Regret for sending me away and for being an absent father in so many ways.) But I couldn't have imagined any place more fun than a horseback-riding academy.

Fun, and *exciting*, actually. It was my roommate, Karen, who introduced me to the daring excitement of doing something against the rules. Probably that's one reason I started smoking cigarettes at school too. A lot of the other kids did it. It was a way to make friends. And Dad would've been thoroughly disgusted had he known part of the weekly allowance he sent me was being spent on those cancer sticks.

Karen walked up to me as I sat in the smoking area one evening. "Will you sneak into the boys' dorm with me tonight, Bobbie?" she asked.

I'd changed my nickname at the beginning of the school year, influenced by "Charlie," another sophomore girl down the hall with a Marine-style buzz cut.

"Sure," I said.

Some other students and I had been drinking Jim Beam, so I felt pretty uninhibited. And Karen was my best friend. She needed my help. How could I say no?

Just before curfew, we stood in the dark behind the tall shrubs next to the brick wall of the boys' dorm. Karen tapped on a window. She had already scoped it out, and her boyfriend, Scott, was waiting for us. He and a friend helped us in. Three others were hanging out on their bunks.

Scott began making introductions when another boy rushed into the room and whispered, "Quick, put them in the bathroom!"

Karen and I were steered into a tight space. The door shut, and pitch black darkness enfolded us.

Karen whispered, "It must be time for room check."

A crack of light shone from under the bathroom door. I shifted around to lean against the wall. In doing so I knocked up against something in the corner. I felt around and realized there were a bunch of *baseball bats* standing there. I jiggled them accidentally with my knee, and the tiny sound of wood knocking against wood reverberated around us as if it were thunder.

"Shit!" I said under my breath. I was sure the baseball bats were going to tumble down any second.........but they didn't.

A minute later the bathroom door opened. Scott welcomed us back into the bedroom with a big smile.

Karen talked intimately with Scott on his bunk. Feeling shy and not wanting to intrude, I just stood there.

Someone gave Karen and I some Jack Daniels, so I went to sit on an empty bunk and sipped nervously, observing the boys in the room. I so wanted one of them to talk to me. I certainly couldn't walk up to one of them and start a conversation. But nothing happened, so I sat there feeling stupidly out of place.

After a while the thought of my biology test the next day prompted me to stand at the window and motion to Karen.

"Come on," I mouthed to her.

She glared at me from Scott's bunk and shook her head no. With my hand on my hip I motioned more insistently. She gave in and we scrambled out the window. Trotting on tiptoe over to our dorm, Charlie let us in the fire escape door.

When we were safely in our room again, Karen griped, "Why did you insist we leave so early? I was having such a good time."

"Oh, well, sorry, Karen. But I've still got to study for my biology exam. It's my first-period class in the morning."

Karen sulked as she got ready for bed.

In the morning I went to breakfast before she woke up. Later, as she crossed the smoking area, I said, "Hi, Karen."

She passed right by me without even a glance, talking with another campus red-haired beauty like herself. Much like the bold, quick-witted Kathleen in my previous high school, with long hair like a shiny, new penny, redheads always seemed so confident. Karen's companion looked back my way as they both laughed about something. Did I hear them making fun of my pimples? My crooked tooth? Karen switched rooms with another girl later that day. I'd never lost a friend before. The sting of that stuck with me a long time.

Fortunately, I had new friends not long after that. My Brazilian roommate was so kind. We wound up pen pals after school ended.

And then there was Beth. She and I would sing into our hairbrushes as we listened to bands like Supertramp on her record player. Their Logical Song worried me though. Would becoming an adult *be* like *that*? But Beth and I didn't discuss the lyrics. Instead we'd take turns using her trunk as a stage, while the one of us on it sang like a super star.

Then too there was the boy who taught me "Nadia's Theme" (the theme song of *The Young and the Restless* soap opera) on the piano. My first encounter with Rick was in the band room one day after the guitar, drum, flute and singing trio I was part of finished practicing. After entertaining us by playing along with his Doobie Brothers cassette, our drummer exited the room. Rick and I were alone.

Rick sat down at the upright piano and

began a song, and I discovered how much I loved piano music that day.

He noticed I was listening and motioned to me to sit next to him on the piano bench. My heart palpitated with the excitement of this tall, handsome and apparently sweet guy's notice of me.

He started playing Nadia's Theme. Once he finished, he asked, "Would you like to learn this song?"

I nodded eagerly, "Sure!"

"Ok. It's not hard."

He demonstrated it slowly for me on the low end of the keys. Then I began to copy his movements on the high end. The romantic mood of that song and my first piano lesson stirred up the emotions of my first crush.

Rick and I often ran into each other in the band room when we practiced and would hang out. I delighted in getting better at "our song", and I didn't rage at myself like I had in Margaret's house whenever I'd made a mistake while practicing my flute.

One night I was playing my sax in the jazz band for our pre-Christmas-break dance. (Because its fingerings are nearly identical to the flute, learning the sax was way easy.)

During intermission, as Rick and I stood outside, he told me, "Bobbie, you're such a special girl. I really like you a lot."

"I really like you too, Rick."

He leaned over and our lips touched. My first sweet kiss. Not like the slobbering French kiss some guy plastered on me once. I was in heaven!

After that sweet, innocent kiss, I didn't see Rick for a while. It turned out that a helicopter had picked him up from the campus. *Was his family that rich?* I wondered. *Will I see him again?* But he never did return.

Liquor and weed became my occasional companions after that. Fortunately, the movie *Go*

Ask Alice scared me away from hard drugs, so I declined them when offered.

But one choice I made was seriously misguided—I accepted a date with one of the local boys and snuck out to meet him after curfew. Sitting in his truck in an orange grove, too naïve to say no, he got me drunk out of my mind to use me to pleasure him. That foul experience turned me off from dating for the rest of the school year.

But I got my mind off that by thinking about the friend I secretly held a torch for. His name was Jason—his nickname, "The White Shadow." A sweet boy with a disarming smile and ready wit. I would have switched places with his girlfriend, Paige, for anything. Why *not* me? Wasn't I blonde and stacked, too? But, no. Instead, he became my dancing instructor. And I learned to love dancing.

None of us imagined what was going to happen to Jason, the only African-American in our school. We had a large contingent of male students from Iran at the academy. Somehow they had gotten it into their heads that Jason had disrespected them. A mob of them decided to confront him at his dorm room. Jason was elsewhere at the time, fortunately, so they only got away with spray-painting graffiti on his door.

But when word spread across campus the next day, that that mob was threatening one of the warmest, friendliest of our students, we were outraged. We wanted the school administrators to address this and protect Jason.

It's interesting to note that as history would have it, the Iranian hostage crisis erupted later that year. Fifty-two people would be held hostage in the American embassy in Iran and would remain so for 444 days until the day our next president, Ronald Reagan, took the oath of office on January 20th, 1981. But as much as the Iranian hostage crisis would soon hold the attention of the world, this problem with our Iranian students and keeping Jason safe held the attention of our student body in early 1979 like his life depended on it. And keep him safe we did.

So now, as my sophomore year ended, all the excitement and freedom of boarding school was coming to an end too. I'd never lived alone with Dad before. And in such a quiet house. But using my turntable and headphones, I didn't notice the quiet much.

Having just quit smoking, I really needed something athletic to put my nervous energy to work. But I didn't realize the necessity at the time. Springboard diving just seemed like a really fun thing to do. I developed discipline that year, rising three mornings a week at five a.m. for weight-room training, then two afternoons a week on the diving board except in the colder months. My efforts even earned me the Most Improved Diver award, although since Dad never attended any of my school events, like concerts or competitions, I didn't go to the award ceremony. I hadn't even known I'd won anything until given the trophy in a big brown paper sack the next day. The news was dampened more by the teacher giving it to me with a disapproving comment. How could I have missed the ceremony? He wanted to know. I hung my head and left.

I was in the marching band, too, when I wasn't on the diving board. So with all this extracurricular activity, it seemed unlikely I could keep my grades high. But my junior year classes were not hard at all. Nothing like the challenge of public school in upstate New York. That wasn't unusual for Florida public schools back then either, I was told.

My senior year became a challenge though, starting when I spaced out in chemistry class. It was like I woke up all of a sudden and didn't know where I was. With a pass to see the guidance counselor, I walked to her office, halfway hugging the walls because I was afraid I'd pass out.

The counselor told my father that afternoon, "Kathy really needs to be seen by a professional, Mr. Richards. I recommend Dr. Feingold. He's helped a number of kids I've referred to him. The best psychiatrist I know in this area."

Dad drove me home in silence punctuated by his deep, heavy sighs. That's how it always was with us. No words. Just sighing.

CHAPTER TWO

But that's not how it was in Dr. Feingold's office. His desk faced the wall. His leather chair faced the overstuffed recliner that I sat in. Toys and children's books laid around the room. A friendly place. A place for opening inner doors.

"You can say anything you like here, Kathy. Whatever's on your mind. It's okay."

His large, curved nose resembled the nose on the actor Basil Rathbone, who played one of my favorite fictional characters in the movies, Sherlock Holmes. But this doctor was short and wide in the hips, not like Rathbone's physique at all in other respects. Somehow his frumpy look put me at ease.

I wondered what his religious beliefs were. Since I was a Christian, it mattered to me a lot to share my faith with him.

"Dr. Feingold. I'm a Christian. Are you?"

"No. I'm Jewish actually."

"Oh," I said.

"That matters to you a great deal."

"Yes, it does." It wasn't just about him knowing. It mattered to me if he was saved or not.

"Don't worry. I believe in God too. My beliefs aren't so different from yours."

Well, they were very different, actually. No, he wasn't saved, so he wasn't going to heaven. That's what they taught us in Sunday school anyway.

Although my mother hadn't been able to raise my brother Brian, four years my senior, and me for much of our childhood due to her alcoholism and manic-depressive illness, she had made sure we were indoctrinated into the beliefs of the Methodist church when we were with her. In one of the places we lived, my afterschool care during the third grade was in the pastoral residence by a reverend's wife. The whole church became my playground that year.

Then there was the West Bend Grotto in Iowa. Created by a devout Christian man and his family, each stone had been imported and carefully laid to pay reverence to Christ and the saints. Mom took my brother and me there numerous times. I loved roaming the Grotto. My sense of devotion to Jesus felt keener there than anywhere else.

So the beliefs instilled in me by the church had me fearing for my psychiatrist's afterlife. But I wasn't there to bring him to Jesus. At least I had been open about my faith. That would have to be enough.

"Thanks for not minding me asking you something so personal, Dr. Feingold."

"Sure, Kathy. I'm glad you asked."

We spent the next few sessions getting to know each other, building trust. It was during the second session that we figured out the pain medication for dry sockets I'd been taking since my wisdom teeth surgery must have prompted the black out and the ensuing problems concentrating. But by our third session, I began going through at least a half a dozen Kleenexes each visit.

I shared with him about Margaret. About crying so many nights when I was little over totally losing contact with Mom because she was too ill to keep Brian and me. About my stomach cramps in bed many nights in Margaret's home that no one realized I was having. About Dad never talking.

And I mentioned my boyfriend, David. We'd been together for over a year, and I didn't understand why I wasn't in love with him. David said little but always quietly listened to me talk and talk about everything under the sun while we sat in his car in the evenings. He told me how special I was and professed his love for me, so why couldn't I love him back, I asked the doctor, hoping for some insight into the workings of my heart.

I told him about how reading Dante's *Inferno* for my classics class was really frightening me. I felt as if I were actually walking through the nine circles of hell with Dante and Virgil. Little did I know that these kinds of hellish feelings would be the norm for me one day.

It was during our sixth session that I began remembering what had happened in my bedroom. Something from which I could absolutely never escape.

"I really hated that stark white, knobby bedspread Margaret put on my bed," I told him. It looked like the popcorn ceilings that were so popular for a while.

"She yelled at me if I didn't I keep it straightened. I always read on my bed, but I never felt comfortable lying on that bumpy thing."

The bedspread that felt cursed. The bedspread that seemed to hate me.

"It only happened in the quiet as I laid on my bed," I continued as I wiped my eyes. I could hardly get the words out. My heart felt like it would burst with the pain of what I desperately wanted to share. "I wasn't trying to hide what happened," I said. "I'd just forget after I left my room." I felt so guilty for keeping this to myself.

As I was about to share my secret for the

first time, I began hyperventilating.

"It's okay, Kathy. You're safe here."

I nodded.

He quickly opened his desk drawer, removed an apple from a small brown paper sack and handed the bag to me.

"Here. Breathe into this as slowly as you can."

I breathed into and out of the bag. After several minutes my breathing normalized.

"Are you feeling better?" he asked.

"Yes. Thank you."

"We don't have to talk about what's coming up for you today. How about next time? Do you want to wait until then?"

"No! I really need to talk about this now. Do we have enough time left?"

"We've got about twenty-five minutes left in

the session. If you think you're feeling up to it, go right ahead."

"Ok," I nodded. I took a deep breath.

"It only happened when I was lying on my bed. I'd be reading a book or daydreaming when a sudden, creepy feeling would come over me. Then I began to hear whispers saying things like, 'You are the most despicable, loathsome, disgusting, awful person in the world. We hate you!' I couldn't always make out the words, but the whispering and hateful feelings towards me seemed to go on forever."

"Oh, Kathy. That must have been so scary," Dr. Feingold said.

"It was."

At the sound of his empathy and concern, I uttered loud sobs without stopping for a long time. I hid my eyes with the Kleenex as my heart exploded with pain.

Dr. Feingold just waited and let it all wash over him. He didn't try to make me feel better. He just sat there and held the space open for me.

On their own, my tears ebbed. I collected myself. I could go on.

"Whatever it was that whispered into my ears was all around me. I couldn't see them, but I was trapped. Frozen with terror, I couldn't move."

"How *awful*," he said.

"But then it got even worse. The voices changed into needles. They pricked me inside. And then I felt like a shrinking balloon losing all its air. These torturous feelings returned over and over again for years. It started about the time I entered middle school. They didn't stop 'til I went away to boarding school. Each time the voices, needles and shrinking finished, I'd forget about it. So it never occurred to me to tell anyone."

"So you've never shared this with anyone else before?" Dr. Feingold asked.

"No. Like I said, I always forgot about it. I didn't mean to."

"You couldn't help it, Kathy. You didn't do anything wrong."

I nodded.

"And this never happened to you after you moved to Florida?

"No." I thought a minute. "Although one time when the pot someone gave me at boarding school made me paranoid, I was really afraid the voices were going to come back. I lay on my bunk waiting, so scared. But they didn't."

The doctor could see I was still thinking. He waited.

"I remember something else about the way I felt after the voices attacked. I remember becoming certain that I'd never be able to hold down a job or take care of my financial responsibilities in any way when I became an adult. That fear still haunts me now."

"So it seems like you lost a lot of confidence in yourself because of the voices and the shrinking feelings."

"Yeah," I said.

"After a while, I didn't read in my bedroom

anymore. I read much less and began watching television alone in the basement living room a lot. It felt like I could escape into the TV and get out of my head. And somehow that was safer."

"I can understand that." He paused. "Wow, Kathy, thank you so much for sharing this with me. It took a lot of courage to share what you did just now."

"Thank you, doctor, for saying that."

It would be years before I found someone to teach me the importance of having courage and how to build it within myself. Neither Sunday school nor public school ever talked about courage. And among kids, having guts is vital. If kids smell fear on you, you can't help but feel ashamed and get picked on for it. I was the one always afraid of the sheep bleating on my grandparents' farm, of the bully in middle school who picked on me on the school bus, of the sound of the garage door going up. The doctor couldn't have known why his compliment meant so much to me, but it sure did.

"Of course. It's true," he said. "It takes guts to open up and explore this kind of intense pain and fear." He paused a moment. "So we've only got five minutes left in our session. Is there anything more you'd like to say before you go or would you like to do some deep breathing exercises until your dad gets here?"

"Breathing, please."

With Dr. Feingold, I didn't mind quietly breathing together. It wasn't anything like sighing.

CHAPTER THREE

The next session, Dad came into Dr. Feingold's office with me. Since I'd seen him a half a dozen times, Dad wanted a report on my progress.

"Kathy is doing some great work here, Mr. Richards. And as you can see from her grades, she's getting her concentration back," Dr. Feingold said.

They talked more while I sat there. I didn't catch most of their conversation since my thoughts had gone off on a tangent about something they'd said. My mind was prone to do this.

Then, all of a sudden, my father was shouting, "Well, my mom...!" But he quickly lowered his voice.

I took it that the doctor had been questioning Dad's relationship with his mother, and he was having none of it.

We left after that. In the car, Dad said, "You're just like your mother and all you need is lithium. But that psychiatrist won't prescribe it for you. You won't be going to see him anymore."

"But, Dad! I need to keep seeing Dr. Feingold."

I was scared out of my wits. I'd just opened up big time to the doctor. I was so vulnerable and still had so much to talk with him about. He was the only soft place to fall I'd ever known.

"Please, let me keep seeing Dr. Feingold, Dad. Please!" I begged.

"You don't need those sessions. David and I have discussed it. We don't think this supposed "therapy" is helping. It's just a waste of time and money."

And there we got to the bottom of it: money (and the fact that Dad disliked the psychiatrist and his methods.) Dad had always been a penny pincher. Mom had told me that many times. And Dad, a well-paid electronics engineer, had to leave the office a little early once a week to take me to those appointments. His time and money were just too valuable to keep doing *that*.

I broke up with David after that. Sure, he'd nursed me after my wisdom teeth operation. For nearly two years, though he rarely said anything, he listened to me endlessly in his car as I used his thigh for a pillow with my feet dangling out the passenger window. I knew he loved me. But I'd led him to get saved, so we were even as far as I could see. He had conspired with Dad to wrench me away from Dr. Feingold, with whom I had felt safe enough to share my sadness, fear and pain for the first time in my life. I would never forgive either of them. Since I couldn't divorce my father, at least I could get rid of the boyfriend who'd betrayed me.

Like all kids though, I had my resilience. No doubt such stamina stemmed, in part, from my appreciation for the tender things wherever I found them. The things that nurtured my heart.

My fifth-grade homeroom teacher, Mr. Wilson, provided me one of my first tender things. Yes, he was incredibly handsome, but it wasn't looks that drove me to buy him cologne for Christmas by saving my twenty-five-cents weekly allowance. (The $2.00 Patty and Gary got from their father every week intensified my second-class citizen complex.)

No. It wasn't Mr. Wilson's looks but the love in his voice when he began reading *Where the Red Fern Grows* to our class that year that motivated me to give him something. During that story my heart just swelled up big with a feeling I'd never known before. Sure, his spelling games were great fun, and his display and discussion of the organs of the human body fascinated me. But the stories he read to us to nurture the development of our character remain among my favorite memories of elementary school.

It's thanks, in large part, to teachers that I kept a bright smile on my face in every annual school picture despite what was happening to me in my bedroom. And other tender things.

Beyond my love for my teachers and learning, even beyond my joy of being transfixed and transported by the imagery and bravery described in the pages of every *Tarzan* novel on my father's shelves, was the nourishment given to me by the lyrics and harmonies on all my record albums. In them I found heart lessons that needed no explanation. Juicy music like John

Denver, America's Children, the Beatles, and the Monkees soothed and saved me from suffering time and again.

Although three of those four bands became famous, it was the unknown fourth, America's Children, that instilled in me an appreciation of other cultures. A gift from my favorite aunt, Jean, the one who selflessly served humanity in India and the United States for the Institute of Cultural Affairs, the record got produced just after she left the band. Incorporating various languages and musical themes addressing ethnic and financial disparities in the world, its folk harmonies nurtured my inborn spirit of compassion to feel concern for the plight of the underprivileged like they were family.

This music informed me of the global-human-family values that my aunt held dear. She couldn't be around in person, but her gift educated and protected me. Knowing my mother's struggle with alcohol, Aunt Jean left me the song "Bottle o' Wine," warning of the dangers of alcoholism long before I hit puberty. No parental lecture or "Just Say No" school assembly could've done as good a job. I've always emulated her compassionate actions for humanity. And she acted on my behalf with this album. There's a reason I call her my favorite aunt.

The musical album, *Mary Poppins*, meant a lot to me too, as it sang of the suffragette spirit for women's rights and the cheery disposition of the kind of ideal caregiver that I had always longed for and would one day wish to be. Recorded books, like *Ali Baba and the Forty Thieves*, taught me the exotic nature of other countries. How fun to find myself trapped inside the cave with Ali Baba and all that treasure where he is so overtaken by greed that he can't remember the secret words, "Open Sesame!"

The warm, fatherly voices of the *Peter Pan* and *Winnie the Pooh* recorded book narrators made their lessons unforgettable. How was I to know that, years later, the book *The Tao of Pooh* would explain exactly what I'd learned as a child from all those lovable characters. Did Pooh Bear wind up influencing me to develop an eating disorder due to his honeypot fixation? No, I would never blame that on Pooh.

In church, the preaching and Sunday school explanations did nothing close to what music did to nurture my beliefs. And being a youngster in the choir of Margaret's small-town Presbyterian church gave me an opportunity to express my devotion. I felt the congregation's love keenest when I sang, "The Red White and Blue" from the "God Bless America" musical album we performed for the bicentennial. Our jolly choir director heard my potential and gave me the opportunity to share my tears of passion during this most moving of musical pieces. The culture of music is hardly something children understand intellectually, but a child's heart can truly develop and soar without limit under music's subtle tutelage.

It was Mom who first introduced me to the elevating power of music during the few years she had been well enough to keep Brian and me after divorcing my father. She was playing *Switched on Bach* the evening we came back to live with her again. Dad had driven us from upstate New York to Iowa, instead of flying us this time, so we'd be able to take all our belongings. Yep, at that point, it looked like I was only going to have to spend second grade in Margaret's house.

We walked in the front door of Mom's apartment, and I couldn't get into her arms fast enough.

"Hey pumpkins!" she said as she wrapped her arms around me first with one of her wonderfully tight bear hugs.

It felt *so* good to be in her arms again.

As we ate a dinner of creamed tuna with peas on toast, Mom had another of her favorite albums, *Jesus Christ Superstar*, on the record player.

"How about we go out to the farm tomorrow?" Mom asked, knowing we'd be delighted.

Grandpa and Grandma's farm was our haven away from the city. Grandpa still raised sheep on it then, and I'd follow those wooly critters down the ravine and up to the pasture land, never getting close enough to scare them since their bleating frightened me more.

We had a whole month of summer left before school started, and Mom couldn't watch us during the week while she was at work. So while she was operating the keypunch machine, Brian and I did our job climbing trees to pick apples and cherries for Grandma to cook with. Why wouldn't we when the pay was so good: we could eat all the fruit we wanted.

But the fun of playing outside on the farm wore off eventually. Many afternoons Brian and I could be found reading from Grandma's extensive library and taking turns napping on the living room couch. No TV was allowed in their home then, even though Grandpa wanted it. So that summer, I began my science fiction period with a cool book about a friendly robot.

The upcoming school year was when I officially fell in love with music. My third-grade music teacher taught us "Inchworm." I loved measuring the marigolds with it. Then she played the album *Peter and the Wolf* for us, and I was hooked. It amazed me musical instruments could tell a story like that, represent characters that way.

Mom's repetitive playing of her *Jesus Christ Superstar* album affected me a lot then too. It had me falling in love with Jesus.

Mom had played the clarinet in school and sang in the church choir. People often told me how much alike Mom and I looked. I had a good singing voice like her too. And despite her difficulties with alcohol and manic-depression, Mom knew how to make me feel loved. I'd picked my instrument, the flute, in fifth grade due to the influence of the six-years-older Patty, whom I idolized. But it was Mom's love and musical talents that had me following in her footsteps singing in the church choir and school chorus every year even though she couldn't be around.

One day Mom had started drinking alone after work. Her time at Cherokee Mental Health Institute the year before, while Brian and I lived with Dad and Margaret, was to help her dry out. Unfortunately, it hadn't had a lasting effect.

Mom called outside to get Brian and me to come in for dinner. She sounded very cross, and we knew better than to keep her waiting when she sounded like that. But after a few more beers, a dinner of soup and sandwiches, and a short nap on the couch, she called sweetly to me. She patted the couch cushion next to her. I sat.

"Kathy, I know you're only eight, but there's something you should know about. It's called menstruation. I realize it's gonna be several more years before you start your period, but it's important you know about this stuff."

She went on to explain about a woman's monthly cycle and something about sex that was over my head at the time. I'm not sure how much sunk in, and I didn't really wonder back then why she went into such detail about it all when I was only in the third grade.

But looking back, I believe she knew she wouldn't be able to keep Brian and me much longer. Too many days found Mom calling in sick, in bed nursing a beer, where severe depression had her immobilized. Brian and I had gotten used to traipsing through the empty field next to our apartment complex to the Tom Thumb burger place for dinner.

I wasn't told in fourth grade when Brian and I had been sent back to live with our father and Margaret again, that Mom had attempted suicide and wound up in the vacant state of catatonic depression in the mental hospital. All I knew is that Dad had hired a carpenter to build bedrooms for Brian and me in the cellar after a monstrous fire had gutted the basement. At the time of the fire, Brian and I had been living what was to become our last year with Mom.

So no matter how much Margaret disliked it, from then on we would be living with Dad and Margaret in her home twenty five miles south of Rochester, New York. And Mom wouldn't become well enough for me to visit her in Iowa in the summers until I hit my mid teens. But I never forgot how Mom talked to me that evening, like a grownup, nor the fact that the pamphlet I got in fifth grade about menstruation and the film the school showed us hadn't been my first lesson on the subject. With great foresight, Mom hadn't left the sharing of the "facts of life" up to Dad or Margaret. A fortunate occurrence since neither one of them even attempted to have that talk with me.

Unable to see Dr. Feingold anymore, I stayed focused on schoolwork and extracurricular stuff, finishing high school and my first year of college.

I began my sophomore year. My newest boyfriend and I had just finished making love for the first time. Out of the blue, I said, "You've got to leave." And I ran into the spare bedroom.

He ran after me. "What's wrong?"

"I don't know. I'm scared! I just need to be alone!"

Kneeling next to the little twin bed where I laid hugging myself and freaking out, he tried to put his arms around me. "Whatever it is, I'm here. You'll be okay."

"No, I won't! Please, get out of here. Just go!" I yelled as I pushed him away and curled up into the fetal position.

We stopped seeing each other after that.

Dad couldn't understand why I was emotionally volatile. I didn't get why at times my temper got so out of control either. Then I missed my period for the second month in a row. A urinalysis confirmed it.

But why was I feeling so paranoid and anxious? I didn't understand it then, but the stress of being a pregnant teen, along with the hormonal changes of pregnancy, flipped me into a major manic episode.

The child's father, the boyfriend who'd broken up with me during the summer, wanted no involvement. And abortion was out. I couldn't end a life and live with that guilt for the rest of mine.

My father's stance was, "If you decide to have the baby, you'd better give it up for adoption. I won't help you if you keep it."

I'd seen how out of control with rage I could get. No way was I putting a tiny, defenseless baby through that.

During mania I didn't have my wits about me either and became impulsive. Growing up without parental nurturing, I was vulnerable and easily influenced by a man's attentions, hoping that sexual intimacy would lead to a relationship or at least companionship. Men found me an easy target to take advantage of.

Mike was different though. He'd carried a torch for me for a year and wanted to be more than my best friend. But how could I be with him when he was giving me unrequited love? Naked in his parents' bed, we stopped within inches of making that mistake. No, he mattered too much to ruin our friendship that way, so instead, a few strangers in bars and twenty-four-hour restaurants benefited from my misguided attempts to find love through the act of giving myself away.

That was until late November. Giving Dad a hard time at home, he locked me out of the house just before Thanksgiving. Tough love. Now was the time, eh, Dad? Mike couldn't understand Dad's strategy. I was four months pregnant.

I wandered through downtown Orlando for four days with no sleep. I became convinced I was the reincarnation of either Mary Magdalene, the Virgin Mary, or the Big Guy himself. Maybe, somehow, all three? I couldn't tell all this to the staff at the walk-in mental health crisis center though. How crazy would that sound, not to mention egotistical?

I checked in, laid on the bench in the waiting room, and dozed off. After roaming the city among strangers, I finally felt safe enough to sleep.

Suddenly a male police officer jostled me awake, shaking my arm. Was I pissed. Didn't they know I hadn't slept in four days?

Don't tug on my arm, I thought. No, I didn't

want to go with them. Why were the *police* harassing me? I needed help, not to be arrested.

Two officers yanked me off the bench. I pulled back and dropped to dead weight with all my slender, five foot, six inches, and 125 pounds. They instantly had me airborne.

Tossed into the back of an unmarked white van like a sack of potatoes, I felt the pain of the bruising caused by the metal cuffs banging against my wrists behind my back. Simultaneously scared and indignant at my situation, I anxiously hoped for psychiatric help rather than jail time.

The cops escorted me through a locked door onto the psychiatric unit of the local Seventh Day Adventist hospital, but the grey, cement-walled cell they locked me in felt anything *but* therapeutic. After I changed into their hospital gown, the nurse sat with me on the bare mattress that lay on a coil-spring bed frame. I didn't realize I was about to be isolated and cut off from everyone. I poured my heart out to her as she handed me a little cup of water and a pill. Along with my racing thoughts came racing speech.

We sat on the bed together for a couple minutes. She listened in her uniform covered with friendly cartoon bears. She smiled and got up abruptly, exited the room, and locked the blue door behind her. She looked through the little six-by-eight inch window at me for a moment and then was gone.

After a while I called out to get someone's attention. A male orderly entered the room. He asked if I had a specific need. I didn't. But would he just stay with me? I asked. No. He backed out of the door the way he came in. Before he could close it all the way, while kneeling on the floor, I grabbed on to his left leg like it was my last chance to remain connected to the human race. If everyone left me, if he left me alone, then it was me, my insane thoughts, and no one else; I knew I couldn't handle that. I held on as tightly as I could and begged him to stay. He yanked his leg free and slammed the door shut in my face. I heard the hard sound of the bolt lock being thrown.

To stop my scary, racing thoughts, I began banging the back of my head as hard as I could against the cement wall. *Maybe I can reopen the scar in the back of my scalp and die*, I thought.

But since accidentally knocking the back of my head against a cement wall so hard I needed stitches hadn't killed me in early childhood, purposely doing it now probably wouldn't work either. I kinda knew that. But what else could I do with my thoughts? So I whammed my head over and over, until at one point I thought, *They're just letting me bang my head. Aren't they watching me with a hidden camera in the ceiling's light fixture? What's wrong with this picture?* And then I got mad.

Well, if the staff won't try to stop me from breaking my skull open, maybe tying this plastic bag around my neck will get them in here. Even in my desperation, I knew I couldn't choke myself to death. But I pretended to try to do it.

No response.

Maybe there isn't any hidden camera, and all they can do is see me through the little window in the door. Damn, if that's the case, then they probably wouldn't like it if I blocked their view. But at least that will get them back into the room to talk with me, I reasoned.

Over to the door went the bed frame, and

up went the mattress against the little window. And yes, the staff did come marching in as expected. But they didn't want to talk with me then, either.

Why not? I'm being nice and apologetic and as friendly as I can be, I thought as they hustled me onto the bed.

As quick as you might rope a calf during a rodeo, the staff tied my wrists and ankles tightly into leather restraints attached to the sides of the metal bed frame. Yes, at this kind of work they were quite efficient. But then, they went away again.

In my short, flimsy hospital gown, I laid on my back, exposed in the crucifix position. That's what I called it anyway. And I couldn't help but think of myself as being crucified, only in a very different way, minus the spikes through the hands and feet, but in a way that seemed akin to how Jesus had been crucified. These kinds of unstoppable grandiose thoughts that felt like heresy swirled around in my brain, intensifying my "crucifixion complex." I had a lot of time to think about such things.

The pill didn't put me to sleep quickly. Left alone in the darkened room, I focused on the traffic light in the street below. Through the metal mesh-covered window pane, as the light changed from red to green then yellow and back to red again, I pleaded with the terror for a long time, praying for release from its vice-like grip on my heart.

There must have been something pitiful in my look as Dad came to visit me after that. As dead set against cigarette smoking as he had always been, he actually gave in to my request and brought me a carton on his next visit.

It also didn't take long for him to have me out of that hospital and flown to Iowa for Mom and her family to take care of me. With Mom, two of my favorite uncles, and favorite aunt driving me, I voluntarily admitted myself to Mom's "alma mater," Cherokee Mental Health Institute. I remained there through the winter until the home for unwed mothers in Orlando had a bed for me.

How I loved it at Cherokee! I wasn't mistreated there; the food was great, and I was among my "peers." Many years later, I would see a documentary of Van Gogh's life and totally get why an insane asylum was the only place he had ever felt safe.

Even though it was a snowy winter, I could walk through the underground tunnels and get anywhere on campus I needed to go with ease. There were group therapy sessions and individual therapy. Music therapy and art therapy. I wrote fantastic poetry (I thought) and journaled a lot. And, so that it wouldn't hurt the baby, the psychiatrist kept me on minimal medication just so I could sleep.

The light medication allowed the energy of my manic phase to continue. I even had a boyfriend and was the most exciting (I thought) freestyle dancer at every dance. Why would I want to leave Cherokee to what awaited me in Florida? I loathed the idea. But soon my pregnancy would be so far along that the airlines wouldn't let me ride. My subdued manic vacation was not going to last. Good thing the high of this mania, with medication taking the edge off, kept me living in the moment. I didn't have to think about Florida or Dad or what would happen with my unborn child.

But the day came all too soon when I found myself in Orlando's Beta House with a slew of other pregnant teens. Sitting in my first house meeting, surrounded by mostly African-American girls, I didn't exactly feel like I fit in. Taking my food stamps on grocery day along with the others, that first walk to the store and back felt like the worst kind of lonely. I tried being friendly, to start up a conversation en route. But I never knew what to say. The result was one cold shoulder after another. My paranoia skyrocketed.

Then my most private things began to go missing. Not just my blow-dryer. My journal and my notebook of poetry. I had to get out of there at any cost. I couldn't afford to have anything else taken from me.

The adoption agency counselor believed me when I called her to say I was going to commit suicide if she didn't get me out of there. I don't know if I would have tried or not, but I knew I needed to be in a place where I felt protected from the world again like I had been at Cherokee. But would I end up back in the hospital where I'd been tortured? I didn't think about that, nor was it my decision to make.

Thankfully, a smaller hospital had the first available bed. It actually had a little garden with plants and fresh air. Despite that though, my heart felt its heaviest. It sickened me that the whole weight of my depression and self-hatred was being hoisted onto the heart and soul of the child in my womb. What a heavy burden my baby had to bear.

I didn't know about Lamaze, had no ink-ling of the labor pain I was in for, and no one was there to hold my hand. I sensed the nurses in the labor-and-delivery unit were rather disgusted by my continually screaming bloody murder for hours until it was time for my epidural.

My daughter, who I'd secretly named Jeruleve by combining the words Jerusalem and Eve, was eventually born in the wee hours of the morning, April 17th, 1983. It was a long walk alone down the hospital corridor to the nursery. I was allowed to hold her once.

CHAPTER FOUR

I moved back in with Dad after the delivery. Six months later, my postpartum/post-mania/post-adoption depression had not lifted. Although I was on psychiatric medication, it only made me lethargic, numb and listless. But still, I needed a job. The Handy Way convenience store around the corner hired me.

I had worked there a month when Dad gave me this ultimatum: "You need to move out by the end of December."

That was a few weeks away.

I moved from a suburb of Orlando to the big city itself. The company transferred me to a store closer to my new home, the Young Women's Community Club. On my minimum wage salary, the YWCC was the only place I could afford thanks to its United Way funding. But I liked living in a dorm room again, and this time I only had one roommate.

At the new store, I fell in love with my new manager, who laughed a lot and taught me the funnest video game in the world—Crystal Castles. That little bear eating up the berries and stealing the honey pot while bees, snakes, and a witch tried to attack him entertained my boss and me in the store every chance we got.

We also hung out at Waffle House with another cashier sometimes, after closing the store. I wound up assistant manager. Eventually, my boss made a pass. I hardly wanted to resist.

Unfortunately, up until then, I didn't know he was married. No wedding ring, of course. I found out eventually, which dredged up a heavy weight of guilt. My Christian moral conscience was strong, but evidently not strong enough to override my infatuation for him (which I thought was love) and end it. Eight months into our affair though, he broke it off, choosing the night of my birthday dinner to tell me. He said his wife was getting too suspicious, and he didn't want to lose the woman who cooked and cleaned and took care of him. *Had he married his mother?* I wondered.

"Doesn't my love mean anything to you?" I asked.

It didn't.

I moved to a different store, but within a year, I was working for a bank as a balancing clerk. Like a Sherlock Holmes detective, only with accounts and numbers. Then I got a second job working part-time at Sea World. It was a rush giving out stuffed animals to children in Shamu stadium and collecting their parents' money, even though it wasn't mine to keep. If it would've paid the bills well enough, I'd have done that full-time instead of the bank job.

But the high life of ample income wasn't to last. Appendicitis struck. My bank supervisor expected me to be back at work within four weeks. The morning I was to return, it felt like a belt was squeezing my rib cage. I called in sick. Another day went by. By the third day, I got the call. I was fired.

I'd already resigned from Sea World before this. I figured two jobs after the surgery would be too much to handle. Now, I had no job, and my roommate (I'd moved into an apartment with a co-worker the previous year) was on my case. *How was I going to pay my half of the rent?* She wanted to know. So did I.

Stress and depression put me over the edge. In a hotel room, I downed all the various psychiatric medications I had with wine-cooler chasers. I laid down to sleep, certain I would be dead in the morning.

I awoke to a banging on the door. I remembered going to the bathroom in the middle of the night, weaving against the bed and the wall to make it to the commode to pee. *Who is banging? Where am I?*

"Yes?" I called.

"Housekeeping. We need to clean the room."

I'd only paid for one night. *Shit! What am I going to do?* I could barely stand up straight.

I don't recall descending the stairs. But I fell hard on the pavement in the parking lot.

Dad and his third wife came to visit me in the emergency room. The nasty charcoal treatment did its job. In the psychiatric unit, after my system had been cleared of the overdose, a guy I'd been dating came to visit me. My roommate had informed him where I was.

I told him I was in trouble. No money. No job.

No problem.

"Why don't you come to live with me in Fort Pierce?" he asked me. He was moving there in a month to start a new job.

Wow! Somebody wants me? How great!

I followed him down there after I was released from the hospital. And, at first, it was all good. But I soon ran out of medication, so severe depression prevented me from getting ambitious enough to look for work. He didn't like me sitting around at home all day while he was working. So, when he suggested I get a job, I said okay but stayed at home all day anyway.

In order to keep up the appearance that I was job-hunting, I moved my car to a place nearby where he wouldn't see it. I'd lay on the couch, day after day, incapacitated by self-loathing, while daydreaming about becoming a stripper. I had a good figure, just not the guts and desperation to try such a job. (Which years later I'd be glad I never did.)

At 5:30 every night, I'd look for him to drive up. That was my cue to race to the back bedroom. All our extra stuff was there. I hid behind the excess furniture and boxes until he started taking his shower. Then I'd sneak out and drive my car back home.

Invariably, his inquiry would be met with, "No luck finding a job today."

One day, he brought a couple of friends home with him for dinner. From my hiding place, I heard them talking and laughing. I couldn't get out to my car, so I snuck into the front bedroom to eavesdrop.

"Yeah, Kathy is so lazy. She's just been sitting around here for weeks. She won't get a job, and she barely helps around the house. It's a good thing she's good in bed."

They all laughed.

"What's wrong with her? Is she just lazy?" one of his friends asked.

"She says she's depressed, but I think she's got a few screws loose. Did I tell you she was in a mental hospital before she came down here?"

"Wow, Joe. You better watch out. You never know what someone like that might do. She could be dangerous."

"Damn, d'you think so?"

One of his friends asked where the bathroom was. That forced me to scuttle quick as I could, like the lowlife bug that I was, back to my hiding place before he caught sight of me. But the gist of the conversation was clear. According to my ex-Marine boyfriend, I was lower than slime.

After that night, I had something else to obsess about besides how worthless I was. *I'm going to get even with him if it's the last thing I do*, I thought. *How dare he talk about me that way behind my back!*

In between soap operas and sleep, I fantasized about how I was going to murder Joe. *He'll be napping on the couch on Saturday*, I strategized. *I'll take the iron skillet. One strong slam to the side of his head with all my might is all it will take.*

After a few days of imagining the scene, I decided to test it out for real. The arm of the couch took the blow pretty well, but the arm of the skillet didn't. Joe never noticed the frying pan was missing its handle. At least not before he kicked me out on Saturday morning.

For several nights I spent the little money I had on the cheapest motel room I could find. The crumbly rat poison I'd sprinkled onto my Wendy's salad didn't do the job I'd intended it to. Now, with no place to stay and the oppressive heat of a Florida summer to contend with, I went to the local mall to cool off one afternoon. Sleepiness overtook me. A closet in the Sears linen area was so deep with so many shelves, I couldn't resist hiding myself in there for a nap.

Unintentionally, I slept until after the store closed. It was dark. No one was around, and I had to tinkle. But if I'd known I was going to trip the silent alarm by crossing the store to the restroom, I wouldn't have. I'd have considered using the drain in the closet.

But since the alarm was activated, I soon heard someone whispering, "Get 'em, boy."

The tinkling of a dog collar assured me a K-9 police team was on my trail. Strangely enough, as I sat encircled by dresses inside a circular display rack, the German Shepherd never even got a whiff of me. He stuck his snout into my hiding place, not more than twelve inches away from my face. I held my breath. Seconds later, they went in a different direction. I was in the clear.

Backtracking to my original hiding place wasn't the smartest decision I could've made though. They'd had it staked out.

I heard those immortal words, "Halt! You're under arrest!"

Three weeks in jail went by quickly though. I asked for psychiatric medication. They gave me some. My depression began to lift, in part because I wasn't alone anymore. I met girls my age and younger, some getting clean from crack. One such girl, four foot nine at most, liked to shout over the cell wall as she stood on the toilet seat. The guys on the other side of the wall whooped and hollered back.

One day, I couldn't take her yelling incessantly anymore. The other fifteen girls in my cell were none too happy about it either. I walked up and tapped her on the thigh as she stood on the commode.

"Would you, please, stop shouting?" I asked.

Next thing I knew, I had the bottom of her foot slammed up against my face. Leaning over me, grabbing onto fistfuls of my hair she jumped down. I grabbed her hair in self-defense and tried to pull her off me. Some of our cell mates got us apart. I walked away with only a sore nose and several scratches on my scalp and ear. I counted myself as lucky. Someone explained to me afterwards that she was in withdrawal. I'd never witnessed the extent to which that can affect a person. And I never wanted to again.

But the days did fly by, in large part because of music. The trustee on our hall had her own cell. It was there that we waited to speak to any visitors that came to see us in the evening. I heard my name called one night a few days after my incarceration began. *Who was visiting me?*

My ex-Marine ex-boyfriend wasn't there to help me in any way. He had just come to see if what he read in the paper was true. It had mentioned my arrest. How embarrassing.

Thanks for coming by to gawk at me, jerk, I wanted to say but didn't.

After he left, I stayed in the trustee's cell with the other five girls, waiting until we all got shuffled back to our big cell. Someone who liked hearing me sing asked me to sing something for them. I sang "Rocky Mountain High" and another John Denver song. Something from the Carpenters, the Doobie Brothers, and Supertramp. The other women, at times, sang or hummed along with me to the songs they knew. A little culture bloomed that night and on other evenings like that one. I felt a little like a star, and time there became bearable.

My public defender got my burglary charge to be reduced to trespassing. I hadn't been robbing the place, but the police suspected I was the "inside girl" waiting in the store until it closed to let my cohorts in. With a stern warning from the judge and, given time served, I soon found myself on the street and homeless again. This time was different though. Worse. Unable to keep up my car payments, my Toyota hatchback had been repossessed while I was imprisoned. Now, I was *on foot* and homeless, a very different scenario.

I walked out of a pawn shop in downtown Fort Pierce minus my precious flute. I'd had it since the fifth grade. But now, I was plus one revolver. As I contemplated where and when I would shoot myself, a guy about my age walked up to me and said hi. Our conversation led me to staying at his place. A neighbor down the street offered to pay me a little money to babysit her fourteen-month-old twin girls.

After a couple weeks, I called Dad. I needed to get away from this set-up. I didn't mind babysitting, but I hardly earned enough to buy groceries. I was stuck in an unknown city among strangers. Dad wired me the two hundred dollars I needed for the beat-up, yellow Chevy Chevette I found. It got me back to Orlando. I left my revolver behind.

CHAPTER FIVE

I drove the 120 miles and arrived on the doorstep of the Orlando Salvation Army. My second step-mother wasn't about to have me stay in her home. And Dad was renting his house to her son, who didn't want a roommate. I'd have to fend for myself some more. I became a frequent flyer at the Salvation Army.

But six dollars a night for a bunk bed in a small room that slept eight was a lot, I thought— it being the 1980's. Especially for someone with no job. And it wasn't easy getting a job with no address of your own. But as I waited in line for the evening meal each night, I kept my ears open. I learned that behind the Salvation Army sat a pond. And around that pond, men trolled in their cars looking to buy time with a woman. I was as desperate as you could get, so with my scruples poking at me I sat by the pond, a long-lasting stain of shame inscribing itself on my conscience.

Thankfully, I only needed to do that a very short time. The receptionist at the Salvation Army took a liking to me. He started letting me stay for free. He even took me with him on vacation.

I'd never been to Fort Lauderdale before. Swimming and fried chicken are all I remember about that trip. And the fun party hat he bought me. It may have been because of his colostomy bag that he never desired or even hinted that he wanted sex from me. He also may have been gay. I didn't know. And didn't care. He treated me with respect and liked having me around. That was a big deal.

After being homeless a couple months, I was able to get a job waitressing at the newly opened Pizza Hut restaurant near one of the hospitals downtown. Yay! I could afford to move back into the Young Women's Com- munity Club again.

I liked waitressing: serving people, chatting it up, and keeping on the move. Good stuff. We employees got to eat all we wanted from the salad bar for free, too. With running to tables and eating salads, I dropped to my all-time thinnest weight. Dad would've thought that was something if he had seen me.

When we were children, Dad weighed my brother and me like a drill sergeant every Sunday for years until he was satisfied our chubbiness had disappeared for good. Our grandparents on the farm in Iowa had fed us a little too well the year Mom tried to take us back, not to mention the junk-food hamburgers we often ate at Tom Thumb. The embarrassment I felt from Dad posting our weights on the refrigerator probably helped the pounds come off sooner. As did the fear he instilled in me when he found out I'd hidden a little bag of potato chips in my room.

So I thought proudly of my trim figure as I left work one afternoon and entered the local ABC bar for a drink. As usual, I felt lonely, so I gladly responded to the attentions of the only other customer in the place. I smiled as he spoke to me, but the music was too loud to hear what he was saying. He motioned me over to sit next to him.

"Hi," I said as I sat on the stool to his right.

"Hi. My name's Rocky. What's yours?"

"Kathy." I paused, nervously trying to come up with something else to say. "Are you a body builder?"

"I work out." His muscles bulged. "Here."

He held up his pasty white arm. "You want to feel them?"

"Okay." I squeezed his biceps. "Wow. They're so big."

His grin revealed bleached white teeth. Were his eyebrows plucked? He appraised me from the corner of his eye.

Neither of us said anything for a few minutes. I began to feel anxious.

"You wanna come over to my place and have a beer?" he asked.

This kind of invitation was not new. Wishing for something other than a one night stand, I'd invariably been disappointed before. *Will it be different with this guy?* I hoped.

I reflected on whether I should ignore the knot in my stomach and go with Rocky. I noticed he was getting up to leave. He appeared put off that I took so long to respond to his invitation.

I quickly said, "Sure. I'll come over for a little while."

He looked at me sideways again and grinned.

He asked if he could ride with me. He didn't have a car. I felt uncomfortable with that arrangement, and my stomach's knot twisted tighter, but I said I didn't mind. Loneliness trumped my intuition.

He lived in a shabby apartment with old furniture and bare walls. In fact, no art or anything of beauty existed in that living room. He handed me a bottle of beer and sat down on the couch close to me. He said nothing for a few minutes, and we drank our beer.

Then *bam*! He plastered a kiss on me. Not one of your sweet and tentative kisses. Not curious and probing. This kiss wanted to devour my entire face! Saliva covered my cheeks, chin, and nose when he was done.

Disgusted, I said, "I need to use the bathroom."

He said okay and pointed the way.

As I walked across the living room, I said

nervously, "I think I'm going to go. I'm pretty tired."

I glanced at him. He didn't say anything.

Upon exiting the bathroom, I stepped into a pitch-black hallway. He was behind me.

"I've got a knife at your throat. Don't scream or struggle or I'll use it."

He pressed the sharp edge of the blade against my throat to make sure I knew he meant what he said.

I've blocked out memories of the pain, the terror, the violence. But not of the things he said afterwards.

Paralyzed with fear, I couldn't get up to leave. He rambled on for a long time about not being of this world. Like he believed he was some kind of angel, or extra-terrestrial, or some other special kind of being. He was really into his narcissistic delusions too. Strange as it seems now, being as freaked out as I was then, my gullibility set in. I couldn't figure out whether to believe him or not.

The next morning, he cooked me breakfast. A fancy one. He told me he worked as a professional chef at the now defunct Rosie O'Grady's Entertainment Emporium downtown. A tourist trap. He spoke to me as if we were dating. Creepy as it might seem to someone looking on, the thought that he and I were dating helped me disassociate from the memory of the violence, much like how I would forget about the torture that happened to me in my mind in childhood. As a victim of rape it's common to feel guilty, ashamed and dirty for getting assaulted, even though the assault is not the victim's fault. But disassociating from memories of the violence diminished those feelings in me, especially if I thought of Rocky as my boyfriend. So, that's what I did.

For the next month, although no sex happened between us, I acted as his chauffeur when he needed rides, and he frequently cooked for me. But when his roommate told me Rocky had another girlfriend somewhere, that was the last straw. I wasn't going to be the *other woman* again. After all, I had my pride, right?

Rocky and I had hung out so much that it didn't occur to me at the time that I should report him to the police. Later that would come back to haunt me, knowing I hadn't acted to protect other women from him. After I stopped seeing Rocky, the shame I felt for going back to him after the assault stung me for years, as well.

Within a month of the rape, my supervisor at Pizza Hut told me I'd better improve my performance. I was making too many mistakes. Customers were complaining. My concentration was slipping.

I switched jobs, but not before a friend at Pizza Hut, a dishwasher with a car-detailing business in his front yard, figured out something was wrong and invited me over to his place to talk. I'll never forget his kindness that night as I cried about the assault. His ebony arms enfolded me for a long time before I left his doorstep. Carrying a debt of gratitude for his kindness since then, I've often wondered if his car-detailing business ever took off.

I hoped to make better tips at Red Lobster, but the size of the giant-sized serving trays looked too intimidating. I was scared I'd drop them and wouldn't be able to remember the menu. I was certain I couldn't cut it there waitressing, so once my two weeks of training were up, I quit.

Since the rape slashed my self-esteem, I felt I couldn't hold down any kind of a job anymore. Convinced I would always be a loser, I slit my wrists. But I didn't know how to do it "right." Instead of dying, I was just panicking. *Why couldn't I kill myself?* I so wanted to die!!! With my wrists wrapped in strips I tore from a white tee shirt, I bought iodine at a convenience store. Tossing it back, I never expected its acid-like burn down my throat and esophagus. Poison control told me a flour and water remedy would work, and it did.

Okay. I was whipped. When neither of those efforts got me even close to death, I talked to the YWCC nurse. She helped me get admitted to the hospital.

This time though, Dad rescued me right away. He flew me to Iowa where I stayed on the psych unit of the local hospital near Mom's place for a couple weeks until I could get into Cherokee.

Always an extensive journaler before this,

writing pages and pages at every sitting, now I barely scribbled two lines a day. No poems. Hardly coherent sentences. No happy dancing. No sex with a boyfriend on the grass. For months, the nurses cajoled me to get out of my bed every morning. It seemed impossible to comply.

After some months on new psychiatric medications, this excellent state-run hospital sent me to a wonderful rehab program. Living in an upscale two-story house with other girls. Group therapies and group exercise. Opportunities to return to college. The greatest kind of program, really.

I lasted there all of two weeks. My paranoia couldn't take sharing a room with five other girls. Everybody was talking about me. I knew they were. And they hated me.

I called Dad. He flew me back to Orlando. We made an arrangement. I could share his house with my stepbrother and live there rent-free until I got a job. Then rent would gradually increase. That was so great of him. I felt very relieved.

Cab driving seemed to be the ticket for me

at that point. I could work whenever I wanted. The evening shift meant I could sleep all day. (My psych meds, on top of the depression, made rising in the morning pretty impossible.) And I could work part-time rather than have an assigned cab five nights a week if I didn't mind waiting for a cab to become available each shift.

Chatting it up with patrons throughout the night kept my mind occupied with something outside of myself. I didn't have to think much about my life or feel the heavy saddle on my heart where devils sat egging me on, "One more time, Kathy. Just try to kill yourself one more time, and you'll probably get it right."

I also liked getting acquainted with the other drivers when we sometimes sat in each other's cabs waiting for fares at the airport, Disney World, or hotel taxi stands—so much so that one cabbie actually nicknamed me "Chatty Kathy" to drive me away. I dearly wanted to make friends. It seemed like I vaguely remembered being able to make friends once, before Rocky. But given that shaming nickname, I knew guys like that cabbie were not interested in anything I had to say. I began to realize other drivers had just one thing on their minds.

CHAPTER SIX

After driving for a year though, I found one man was different from the rest. He seemed engrossed with reading some kind of newspaper whenever I saw him at the station waiting for his assigned cab. Terry and I began hanging out now and then, sometimes having a beer together or just talking. He was married, I knew, and totally off limits. But I didn't see him that way, anyway. Not like a love-interest. Terry was a real, honest-to-goodness friend who cared about me. I couldn't remember the last time I'd had one of those.

We'd known each other about a year when, one hot night in June, he invited me to sit with him in his cab and stay cool while I waited for a cab assignment. I was miserable as usual. I'd just tried for the umpteenth time to kill myself earlier that week using a combination of a medication overdose and carbon monoxide poisoning in the closed garage of my father's house. The car fumes were too strong for me to sit there, and my pills just made black dots appear before my eyes. So there I was after yet another failed suicide attempt, desperate for someone to pull me out of the depths.

Terry listened attentively for a long time. It seemed like I'd talked to him and cried about everything under the sun that night, and nothing was likely to cheer me up. Then, out of the blue, he made a suggestion that was totally foreign to me, something truly unconventional. He offered me a simple method I'd never heard of, one he assured me was a powerful enough tool to change my plight. I was intrigued.

Early in my manic pregnancy, I had met "Dare to Be Great" motivational speaker Glenn Turner at a Sambo's restaurant. (Yes, in an area where the KKK still occasionally parades through downtown Orlando, this restaurant's name stuck for a long time.) Riding in his car, Turner told me how he'd made another young woman into a beauty pageant winner and hinted he could do the same for me. That surprised me because I never saw myself as attractive. I hung out with his get-rich-quick, multi-level-marketing gang, while my hyper-manic imagination convinced me one of the men in the group who was pursuing me for sexual favors was communicating with me telepathically.

After this car ride, I told Dad what Mr. Turner had said. As rare as it was for Dad and me to talk together, I'll never forget how he sat me down and straightened me out about con men real quick. I didn't mix with Turner and his group after that, and Turner was eventually sentenced to seven years in prison for using an illegal pyramid scheme to bilk people out of thousands of dollars.

One thing stuck with me that Glenn Turner used to say. He shared a fable. The theme of the fable was "Anything is possible in the land where anything is possible." As the gullible, naive girl I was, over the years I often wondered about that. Is it possible to live where anything is possible? For many years, I also couldn't figure out whether the magic steps portrayed in the roof-hopping scene in the movie *Mary Poppins* were really made out of magic or not. That shows you how gullible I was for much of my life.

Now, in Terry's car, after it felt like every hope in me had been pulverized to dust, and I had tried, yet again, to throw away my life with another suicide attempt, he encouraged me to hope anew. But Terry wasn't a charlatan. He was no con man. He was the only friend I had in the world. And I knew I could trust him. I held on to what he gave me that night. Something as easy as singing a simple song. I held on to it for dear life. And I ran.

I ran to the literature he gave me. And I studied voraciously. Not only the theory, philosophy and practice at the heart of this method. I became exposed to Emerson and Thoreau and read about the Enlightenment period and the Renaissance artists. About the relationship between Socrates and Plato. About the lives of Florence Nightingale and Joan of Arc. About the spirit of the Declaration of Independence, the Statue of Liberty, and the origin of Mother's Day.

I learned about the universality of Buddhahood, that everyone equally possesses the potential to attain enlightenment in this lifetime. Prior to his teaching of the Lotus Sutra of the Wonderful Law, the historical Buddha, Shakyamuni, taught according to the customary thinking of his day, saying that women could not attain enlightenment. Only in the last eight years of his life did he teach in the Lotus Sutra[2] that the enlightenment of women was possible. And not just possible. The first to attain enlightenment upon hearing Shakyamuni's teaching of the Lotus Sutra was an 8-year-old girl. She showed all the proud men of learning what was what, which of course infuriated the arrogant ones. Nothing could have convinced me of Shakyamuni's compassion more than his teaching of the enlightenment of women first in male-dominated, ancient India.

I also became inspired by Thoreau's writings and poetry like Daisaku Ikeda's *Joy of Living*. I began to believe I had it in me to develop a profound and joyous state of life, to even make my life a masterpiece like a great Renaissance artist.

I learned that the foundation of this music-like method Terry shared with me is a philosophy rooted in how to live a correct way of life. At meetings, I saw incredible examples of people living contributive lives, creating good fortune and happiness. I learned that no one could give me happiness. To create joy in the depths of my life and achieve anything remarkable, I had to become strong. And to do this, courage was indispensable.

And this made sense to me, knowing fear so well. Now, I had a way to develop courage and extricate myself from the muck and mire of fear and anger masked as depression. Stevie Wonder sings a song with the words, "If you believe in things that you don't understand, then you suffer. Superstition ain't the way." Now, through studying something that manifested as a kind of great common sense, I began challenging my ignorance and suffering, and gradually developed a clear understanding of *why* things happened to me. Day by day, I began to feel a little less clueless and a little more clued in to the workings of life, a little more hopeful, and a lot more empowered to take charge of my destiny.

These works of literature weren't just self-help books, and this wasn't simply a self-help method or new-age technique in chakra balancing, self-hypnosis, or subliminal reprogramming. I had tried those. They may have helped others, but they didn't help me change *my* life. Not for the long haul, nor did they give me a reason or motivation to change inside either.

Neither was this something requiring my

seclusion from society in a monastery or some-thing only yogis and monks had all the time in the world to do. This was a practice for ordinary people.

Terry introduced me to his friends. Their eyes shined with joy as if the sun rose in their hearts every day. Their cheerful voices lifted me. I heard things like "making the impossible possible." Could it be true? I sensed they saw something precious in me that I couldn't see in myself. Songs they'd sing, like "The Impossible Dream," resonated with me. Doing what's right, no matter what, for justice and truth.

The circumstances of my birth and so much that came after it cemented a sense of utter powerlessness in me. In my quest through var-ious meditative practices, Theosophical Society meetings, and church pews, I never imagined I'd find a teaching that would actually empower me to transform my life from deep down within. Like many people, I was thoroughly indoctrinated in the belief that the mere fact of my birth as a mortal meant I was guilty and needed to be saved and forgiven for my wrong-doing. It was pounded into my head that someone or something above and beyond me held the power to save me, but saving myself from suffering wasn't even on the table for discussion. So if I supplicated like I was supposed to, towards that which held the power, I would avoid suffering for all eternity. If I maintained this attitude until the end of my life, I'd be good enough to get my reward after I die. But though I swallowed this belief hook, line, and sinker, I never felt good enough or good about myself.

Don't get me wrong. I'm very glad I was brought up Christian. It made me feel that somebody loved me and was always thinking of me. I had something to be passionate about that developed my innate goodness and taught me morality. I developed a conscience with strong scruples, and I cared about people. But having experienced so much trauma, long before I ever met Terry, I'd stopped feeling that there was a Power that cared about me.

I tried many Orlando and Central Florida churches for a few years after moving there. But I found none of those had ever made me feel welcome like I'd felt in my small-town New York Presbyterian church. And with no support through the terrible times, my foundation of faith kept crumbling. *Was this Power and heaven even real?* I questioned.

The book *Illusions* by Richard Bach suggests that when we become enlightened to the truth of life and let go of what holds us down, we can then help others do the same. I liked the premise of the book a lot at the time I read it, but it didn't tell me *how* I would go about becoming enlightened. The practice Terry shared with me of the strategy of the Lotus Sutra to bring forth my Buddha nature utilizing the Mystic Law of cause and effect not only showed me how, but also taught that I didn't have to wait to help others who were suffering. Even as I strove to overcome suffering and accomplish my greatest dreams, I could encourage another person with my hopeful struggle just as I was. In fact, helping another was indispensable to my own happiness and a source of great joy. The Bodhisattva spirit[3] in me began to thrive.

My favorite philosophy teacher once said that each of us is the protagonist of our own life, each the hero or heroine of his or her own story or play on the stage of our lives. But every time those psychotic episodes happened in Margaret's house, an invisible trapdoor in the floor of the stage of my life kept being yanked open under my feet. Each time another trauma happened, I fell deeper into the black abyss beneath that stage. I fell so deep into the darkness that eventually the only light I could see from where I landed was like the pinpoint of light coming from a star in the night sky.

In junior high, I starred as a puppet in the musical *Pinocchio*. I performed "When You Wish Upon a Star." That song promised my dreams would come true if I only wished for them. I memorized those lyrics with longing. It was the only hope to hold on to then.

But now, I had something I could actually *do* to *create* hope and to change myself and my circumstances. Singing the song "The Impossible Dream" with others, I began to believe in a better world and that, by becoming a happy person of noble character, I would actually be changing not just my own destiny but also the destiny of humanity, a concept referred to as human revolution. I didn't have to wait to go to heaven to know what happiness was. My new purpose in life? To become unbelievably happy in this lifetime and help others do the same. To create world peace by empowering one person after another. A long way to go about it, but has any other process led to world peace yet? Now, instead of looking up longingly from that deep, dark abyss, I began to believe I could even reach that star in the night sky.

CHAPTER SEVEN

But attaining supreme enlightenment in this lifetime wasn't exactly going to be easy. Nor would it be quick. Transforming my life from one of deep suffering to profound joy would take a while. But from the beginning of my practice, because my Buddha nature started attracting good experiences into my life, I began manifesting the things I needed or wished for like I had never been able to before.

People's generosity towards me spilled forth. For example, a trip I'd been wanting to go on but couldn't afford was given to me for free. Someone I'd just met through a newspaper ad trusted me with their car for free for as long as I needed it during the trip. The lawyer who'd won a settlement for me elected of his own accord not to take his fee so that I could keep all of the money. And a conversation with a co-worker in which I casually mentioned how I'd always loved the star sapphire Mom had worn led this woman who barely knew me to surprise me with a platinum star sapphire and diamond ring she'd been keeping in her jewelry box. How special to be given such a meaningful gift—one that could remind me of Mom. I'm grateful for each of these generous people and their kindnesses. They were some of the proof of this practice working—even eliciting these kinds of positive responses from people in my environment. What a new experience for me!

I also began attracting the kind of meaningful, nurturing friendships within and outside of Terry's group that I'd sorely needed for a long time. A wish-granting jewel existed inside my life. It always had. I'd just never known how to activate it before.

This newfound hope made me believe things could always get better. As a result of practicing this teaching of the sanctity of life, I never attempted suicide again. It began to make sense that the way I died and the predominant life-condition I exhibited in life would be the determining factors in what I would experience after death. I didn't know what deep happiness felt like yet, but I wanted to find out rather than die miserable at my own hand. Still, it would be years before I stopped longing for death.

Then one day, I read something that gave me the not-so-bright idea to stop taking my psychiatric medication and cure myself of my disorder without telling anybody what I was doing. I'd surprise them all with the big change in me.

A big change happened all right. One day, Terry sat me down and said, "Kathy, I don't know how to tell you this. From what I've read, I understand that when women have been raped, it can tend to make them really angry, even rageful. And Kathy, as much as I care about you, I don't feel like I can be around you anymore. It's just too hard to handle your anger."

My heart sank. I didn't know what to say except how sorry I was. Terry and I didn't hang out after that. I only saw him at work or when the group got together. But I couldn't blame him for feeling that way. I knew I was hard to be around.

To others, off my medication, I was ir-ritable and short-tempered without much aware-ness of it. By myself, I was throwing things through the window, pounding my knuckles as hard as I could against my head, and pulling my hair. My tantrums had gotten loud. Arguments between my stepbrother and me got to the point that he moved out.

Then there was work. One night at the county fairgrounds, waiting for a fare, a sea of people surrounded my cab. One black youth about sixteen-years-old bumped the back of my car. I stormed out of my cab, grabbed him by the tail of his sweater, and swung him around. "You're paying for that if there's a dent in my cab!" I screamed.

Police cars came in our direction. I slunk back into my cab, lucky to get out of there before the cops investigated or I got hurt.

But more trouble followed. Other cabbies complained to management about my temper. I was soon pounding the pavement for a new job.

I still never explained to anyone that I was off of my meds. Not even to friends I'd become close to in Terry's group. One friend whom I told about my disorder asked me if it wasn't possible that, when I thought of myself as some re-incarnated savior in my psychotic episodes, my inherent Bodhisattva spirit was trying desperately to awaken in me. The Bodhisattva spirit to save others from suffering and impart joy. She certainly had an enlightened perspective about my experiences that had never occurred to me before.

And there was the friend in Terry's group that had immediately taken me under her wing and listened to me endlessly for hours whenever I needed her, accepting me unconditionally. I'd never known what it meant to be mothered until I met Kayuni. But I never even told her my secret—that I'd stopped my medication. Even when she surprised me with groceries after I got fired from the taxi company. Unbeknownst to her, those groceries kept me from creating the bad karma of stealing food like I had in similarly desperate circumstances years before. No, I didn't tell my secret to anyone at all.

But being off medication meant I had my energy back. I could get up at a decent hour and find a job. Even work full time again. I began cashiering at a Mobile gas station. I didn't mind it, being behind the safety of a bulletproof window at night. But our dictator-like boss was something else.

We nicknamed him "little Napoleon" because of his height and demeanor. After nine months, he and I actually almost came to blows. I should've sued him for harassment. But again naïveté entered the picture so I didn't know his calling me out behind the station to duke it out with him was harassment. Nor did I back down. He wasn't going to intimidate me. I walked out there with him. But at the last minute, just as I anxiously thought our fists were going to start swinging, he backed off. Instead, he fired me the next day, citing "insubordination." Yeah, I could have sued. But what did I know?

After writing a letter to one of the owners of the taxi company and talking things out with him, I was rehired. I drove for a few months. But being off of medication for over a year took me to that dangerous place. Unable to sleep again for four days, I called Dad. He witnessed my chaos. Clothes, mail, and so much else were strewn across the floor throughout the house.

"I'm having problems again, Dad. I'm going to drive myself to the crisis unit." Asking him to drive me there seemed out of the question. But I couldn't make simple decisions for myself at that point. "Would you help me pack some things?"

I didn't go into detail with him about what

was happening in my mind. I knew he wouldn't be interested anyway. Like how the TV was giving me personal messages. I was on a mission for the government. They had hidden a nuclear bomb in my chest. That's why I felt such intense heat there. And scared? How scared would you be if you thought you had a nuclear bomb in your chest ready to explode at any moment?

A friend I'd recently introduced to Buddhism had begun experiencing its benefits. In my disordered mind, I couldn't comprehend that what I felt inside was really the sunlight of Buddhist compassion rising in my heart for the first time—not a bomb.

After a lengthy detour into a local church where I sat alone at a piano enjoying the feeling of a spiritual presence there, I finally arrived at the Sanford Crisis Unit. One of the technicians took me on a little tour of the facility. I say little, because it was cramped. Ten rooms with the capacity for three patients to a room. The dining area doubled as a craft area, a group therapy area, and a TV room. A medication window, a small consult room, and a locked office surrounded by observation windows filled out that end of the facility. At the other end of the short hall was an observation desk with several TV monitors. Once the bedrooms were locked for the day, everyone could be seen with ease from either location.

As soon as the tour was over, my nerves started clamoring for a smoke. I asked the technician, "Can I have a cigarette?" No one had shown me where the smoking area was yet.

"You'll have to wait until smoke break," she said with her Filipina accent.

"How long will that be?"

"I don't know. Not long probably. We have smoke breaks every two hours. Don't worry about it."

Easy for her to say. I might have to wait an hour or longer to have a cigarette. I was jonesing here!

"Really? How long do you think that will be?"

She was checking her shirt pocket for the cigarette pack she always carried. "I don't know exactly. Just wait."

Another short, dark-haired woman like Margaret with a bit of a dictator complex.

I thought, *Well I'm not taking this shit.*

I grabbed the pack of cigarettes from her pocket. She shouted for help, and all hell broke loose. I was quickly airborne by two tall, beefy men and carried to the seclusion room. A six-by-ten foot, fake-wood-paneled room behind a locked door.

I sat on a bare, plastic mattress placed inside an immovable wooden base. I got used to the idea that I had to stay put and remembered the one essential phrase Terry had given me. So I recited it with my back to the door and its little window, to ignore the onlookers.

Soon I was sitting on the floor, playing with a cup of yogurt someone had brought me. Though I'd abstained from sex for several years, I was convinced that the bulging in my lower abdomen was a baby. I speculated it might have been an immaculate conception. Then my manic-fevered mind thought, *I'm having a pop music superstar's baby!* I mused over who it might have been. It all seemed very plausible.

Then as I sat on the floor I began rocking. My arms around me in the form of a self-hug, I sat doubled-over on top of my crossed legs. Just rocking.

The staff entered in a rush and grabbed me. In seconds, leather restraints were around my left wrist.

I knew where this was heading. "Please, don't put me on my back. Anything but that. I was raped at knifepoint a few years ago. I just can't handle being tied down on my back. Please!"

They agreed and tied my wrists and ankles so I was lying on my stomach. So it was okay. My abdomen wasn't exposed. Somehow that wasn't scary.

After half an hour or so, I called out through the closed door, "Excuse me. I have to go to the bathroom."

Some minutes went by, and a tech came in with a bedpan. With two other techs in the room helping, they turned me over and then re-tied just one wrist so I could urinate. When done, how- ever, and the bedpan was removed, they kept me on my back and retied my other appendages that had been loose.

"Please, don't leave me like this. I need to be on my stomach. Please!" I pleaded and screamed for them to help, reminding them of the effect of the sexual assault that made this position petrifying. Over and over, I screamed in terror.

One of the medical staff entered and injected me with something. She didn't respond to my pleas either, closing the door as she left. As I begged and cried, I noticed one technician seemed to be unable to take his eyes off of me from the little window. Such beady, pitiless eyes I'll never forget. I pleaded with those eyes for mercy but might as well have been asking the dots on the wall for help that a short while ago had been talking to me.

Hours later, I awoke in another room in darkness. It felt like I was still tied down to a bed, but then I realized I wasn't. Completely paralyzed by fright, I couldn't move my body even an inch. For a long time, I tried to move, motivated by the need to talk to someone. I also attempted to call out but could not make a sound.

Finally, with all my strength, I shrugged my right leg over the side of the bed. I rolled my body over in such a way as to be able to push up with my arms from the mattress. I slowly navigated my ten-thousand-pound body to the door and out into the hallway. I motioned to the nurse at the observation desk. I'd not seen him before.

He came up to me and asked what I needed. I tried to speak, to make words come out, but couldn't. Seeing me put my hand to my lips and then my throat, he understood that I couldn't speak. He led me into a consultation room where, again, I tried to speak. The more I tried to talk to him, the more my throat constricted. I felt like I was suffocating. He said it would be okay, that I'd be okay.

But my fear only heightened. I felt like the woman in the movie, *The Tingler*. It was the only movie I watched as a kid that made me have nightmares. In the movie, Vincent Price plays a mad scientist who tries to gaslight his wife by placing a giant centipede-like creature, the one he had created in his laboratory, in her bedroom while she's sleeping. During the night it enters her body so its pulsating antennae-like pincers could squeeze her wind-pipe. She's not killed by the creature but is only prevented from speaking. The husband's goal was to scare her to death. This is how terrified I felt.

Some friends said they came to visit me shortly after I was admitted there. One told me how I had been sitting at a table with her, saying I was writing a letter. But I had no pen to write with and no paper to write on. Probably due to the heavy Haldol anti-psychotic sedation, I have no memory of their visits at all.

But I do recall bits of a phone conversation between Kayuni and me once I was coherent and able to speak again. I'd worried ever since I began practicing that I might've been doing wrong in God's eyes. So if some religious zealot had told me that what happened to me in that seclusion room was "God's punishment for straying away from Him," I would have prostrated myself on the floor and begun begging for forgiveness. In fact, that's exactly what I thought. I shared this with Kayuni. As a result, I sensed she began sending me courage and hope with her Buddhist practice, like invisible radio waves were penetrating my heart as if no distance existed between us at all. If not for her support, I can only imagine the person I would've become after that. Within two weeks of the night I was struck mute, I began my spiritual practice and study anew, never stopping since.

Although I'd had three months of intensive inpatient treatment, I was far from being able to take care of myself. So I was given a room across the street in a newly built rehabilitation home. I remained there for one year, attending an out-patient treatment center during the week. Its director, Bob, his wife, and some other great counselors helped me get myself together. Class-es taught me to understand bipolar disorder better, as well as how to cope and improve my people skills. Smoke breaks at the outdoor picnic tables allowed for socialization, but mostly with people like me who had little to say being that we were all in something like a trance from the drug sedation. Fortunately we went on outings now and then, which made me feel a little more normal.

I didn't have my car for quite a while but wanted to go to Buddhist meetings. The name of the sangha (Buddhist community of believers) that Terry had introduced me to is called the SGI-USA. SGI stands for Soka Gakkai International, which means international value-creating society. So while I couldn't drive, one little, elderly yet youthful Japanese lady picked me up for SGI meetings regularly, and I fell in love with the sound of her happiness and sweet laughter ringing in the car on every trip. Would I become happy like that one day? Though I couldn't do it morning and evening every day, with much support from such friends, I continued my spiritual discipline to the best of my ability to transform suffering into happiness.

The swelling in my abdomen turned out to be tumors. The doctor decided a hysterectomy was unavoidable. I had the surgery and stayed on psych meds. Due to the effects of the trauma, hysterectomy and meds, for the first time in my adult life I ballooned into obesity. But, after a year of working towards independence, I landed a full-time job again.

CHAPTER EIGHT

I really liked registering patients into the hospital. They commented that I'd make a good psychologist because I always listened thoughtfully to whatever my patients had to say.

Three years later, I was still going strong at the hospital. I hadn't wanted to stay at my job that long, but Kayuni encouraged me to. She said it would help me develop character and depth as a person. I wanted that more than anything, to develop the kind of compassion this woman demonstrated in her care and concern for others. It wasn't my dream job, but I knew I was growing.

Then one day, I had a chance to use my temper and sense of justice for good. Our newest shift supervisor often left the hospital for hours, sometimes not returning for the rest of the shift. Problems invariably arose that we needed his help on. None of our previous female supervisors had ever left like that, and it wasn't right. Although I approached my coworkers about this, no one else was willing to say something to management about it. For months, we just did the grin-and-bear-it routine.

Then one night, he and I disagreed about something. He lost his temper and yelled at me to clock out. I felt a passionate fire ignite in my chest, but as hard as it was to hold my tongue, I said nothing and went to leave. Then he changed his mind and said I should stay. I told him I'd already clocked out and was leaving. He said that if I left, I was fired. Although uncertain, a part of me didn't believe he had the authority to fire me. So I went home.

Instead of taking this lying down like I always had and giving in to fear, hopelessness, and victimhood, I decided to make this an opportunity to transform things at work for everyone's benefit. My anger towards the shift supervisor strengthened my motivation to use my practice to win. Then the anger turned into compassion as I set my intention for my shift supervisor's happiness and the greatest happiness of the staff and determinedly prayed to appreciate him and the situation I found myself in.

I called the next day and asked my department head to arrange a meeting between herself, the shift supervisor, his supervisor, and me. How anxiety-provoking! I was the "little guy" about to go barehanded into the lion's den. How could I possibly face my three superiors and come out of the department head's office a winner? My spirit to fight against authoritarianism emboldened me. A spirit I developed as one of ten million lay-believers "excommunicated" by a corrupt high priest of a Buddhist sect bent on controlling its membership for its own gain.

In 1991, the High Priest of Nichiren Shoshu, a small Japanese Buddhist sect that had been supported financially by the Soka Gakkai, sought to confuse our lay membership into leaving the SGI and joining the temple. The High Priest believed this unprecedented excommunication would increase the priesthood's monetary support by increasing the number of temple members it had direct control over. He even had a particular number of members in mind, two hundred thousand. This would be the number of people the High Priest expected it would take to fund the lavish lifestyles the priests had become accustomed to.[4]

After excommunicating us, the High Priest's true nature came to light in part because one brave woman came forward with knowledge exposing his ignoble tendencies and, also, due to the firsthand accounts of pure-hearted reformist priests who left Nichiren Shoshu and spoke out against the shenanigans of the High Priest and his cronies. Those who left the sect told of abuses they'd endured as young acolytes in the hierarchical priesthood system where the egalitarian nature of Buddhism was nowhere to be found. Not long after the excommunication, the High Priest further showed his spiteful colors by destroying an architectural wonder built by the sincere donations of millions of lay practitioners.

It was largely due to the educational initiatives of the president of the SGI, Professor Daisaku Ikeda, who was maliciously criticized by the priesthood, that we were able to see through its machinations. We were studying about authoritarianism long before the excommunication occurred, including how throughout the history of Buddhism, starting with its originator, Shakyamuni Buddha, corrupt individuals have tried to take advantage of pure-hearted practitioners. With the aim of taking control of the Buddhist order, Shakyamuni's own cousin tried to kill Shakyamuni and incited the king of Magadha to severely persecute Shakyamuni and his disciples.

Humankind has suffered through count-less harsh lessons in authoritarianism, such as Hitler and the Holocaust, the Jim Jones cult's mass suicide, and more recently, the 9/11 attacks. The insidious influence of the three poisons of greed, anger and foolishness ex-pounded in Buddhism is truly frightening! Although a dark chapter in the history of Bud-dhism, study and discussion about the priest-hood issue and our excommunication helped our spiritual community learn to recognize the tendency for arrogance and authoritarianism in ourselves and others and transform ourselves and the situations we find ourselves in for the better. This became a great catalyst for our growth, and our organization became more hu-manistic and compassionate in the process. It certainly prepared me for the situation I now found myself in.

Of course, compared to horrific atrocities, my shift supervisor's actions were seemingly insig-nificant. But I recognized his authoritarian ten-dencies and knew that leaving things the way they were would only allow him to keep causing problems. So using my Buddhist practice, I armed myself with courage and the spirit to honor the Buddha nature in my three superiors and entered my department head's office to speak my truth. The four of us barely squeezed into the little office.

Larry, the shift supervisor, began, "Kathy left work without my permission. She didn't follow my instructions. That's what I call in-subordination."

"But don't you remember, Larry, you told me to clock out?" I asked. "You lost your temper and actually yelled at me to clock out, so that's exactly what I did. Then you changed your mind and told me I should stay. But I wasn't on the clock anymore, and because of the way you treated me, I needed to go home and cool off rather than stay. I was just following your original instructions. I thought that was the best thing to do at the time."

The department head then interjected, "Is that what happened Larry? You told Kathy to clock out and go home?"

"Well, yes, but..."

"It seems to me that Kathy did what she was told. Why did you tell her to clock out in the first place? That seems rather extreme."

"She was getting huffy with me."

I said, "You know that's not what happened, Larry."

I looked at the department head who seemed all ears to what I had to say. "What happened was one of my patients in a lot of pain had been sitting in the lobby for several hours waiting for a bed. He was really suffering. I had called and asked Larry to talk with the bed management office about speeding up the process of getting my patient into a room, but Larry has this thing about calling bed management. It seems he doesn't like to do it. And the rest of us are not allowed to. Finally, I walked around to the ER registration area where Larry was sitting and asked him about it. He told me not to give him a hard time, and I asked him why he wouldn't just make the phone call. That's when he yelled at me to go clock out. That's basically what happened."

"Is this true, Larry?" my department head asked.

"Well, yes, basically. But..."

The department head interjected again, "So after you told her to clock out, then what happened?"

Larry appeared speechless, so I answered her question. "Well, after I clocked out and was walking to the door to leave, Larry told me I should stay, that if I left I was fired. But he doesn't have the authority to fire me, does he?" I paused a moment, and it looked like the department head shook her head "no" ever so slightly. But she didn't say anything.

So I went on, "I also want to bring up the fact that Larry is often not around the department when problems come up. He frequently leaves the hospital for hours at night. The rest of us are left short-handed while the person he leaves in charge gets overwhelmed. This has been a problem for quite a while now, and since we're all here discussing problems, it seems the time to bring it up. I hope that's okay." I looked at the department head questioningly.

She nodded with pursed lips.

Everyone got quiet. Larry's eyes shot poisoned darts at me. After a long pause, the department head thanked me for coming in and said I could go back to work.

I don't know what else was discussed, but those three sat in there for a long time before I saw them again.

What I do know is the result. Larry got transferred to a much smaller hospital, and his supervisor, the woman who always seemed to shy away from taking responsibility for or helping us with anything, decided then and there to take early retirement.

I kept my job, and most importantly for everyone was our wonderful new shift supervisor, Tom. A short, friendly, warm dude with a human-istic approach. He treated everyone with respect and kindness, helped everyone in every way he could, and boosted morale off the charts. With the situation transformed, I now had amazing actual proof that this Buddhist teaching of chant-ing the one essential phrase, *Nam-myoho-renge-kyo*[5], works to make the impossible possible.

So now, as to the core of this practice. The phrase *Myoho-renge-kyo* is the title of the Lotus Sutra of the Wonderful Law as it was translated from Sanskrit. And like the way every individual is like an interesting book and a person's name represents everything about that person, this title, *Myoho-renge-kyo*, is the heart and essence of the entire twenty-eight chapters of the Lotus Sutra.

In English, *Nam-myoho-renge-kyo* has various interpretations and depths of meaning, but it generally translates as:

Nam devotion/to fuse with
myo wonderful/mystic/unfathomable
ho law/dharma/phenomena
renge lotus flower/cause and effect
kyo teaching/sutra/sound.

There's great significance in *renge* meaning lotus blossom. A lotus flower blooms and drops its seeds at the same time symbolizing the simultaneity of cause and effect. A lotus grows in a muddy swamp symbolizing the delusions and troubles of our ordinary lives, while the blossom symbolizes Buddhahood, which blooms out of our lives but never touches or gets sullied by the mud. Also, in addition to mystic, wonderful and unfathomable, another three of the many varied meanings of *myo* is to open, to revive, and to be fully endowed.

Put simply, *Myoho-renge-kyo* means the Mystic Law of cause and effect that permeates the universe through sound. According to this universal law, our experiences, circumstances and tendencies, our karma, is created by our causes—our thoughts, words and actions in this life and in past lives. Chanting *Nam-myoho-renge-kyo* aligns us with this law, the essence of the Lotus Sutra, which says that everyone equally possesses the Buddha nature and can bring forth their fundamental enlightenment from within. Through chanting, one develops a more noble character, infused with the qualities of a Buddha, including great wisdom, boundless compassion, courage, infinite hope, confidence, strength, perseverance, vitality, deep gratitude, profound dignity, warmth, humility, and undefeatable happiness. Chanting changes one's karma and destiny for the better, transforms sufferings into happiness and good fortune, and moves one towards the realization of one's greatest dreams.

Feeling victorious at the hospital, I knew

the most difficult part of this battle, the struggle to win over myself, had been won way before I entered my department head's office. Not only did this Buddhist philosophy encourage me to overcome these problems instead of being overcome by fear and self-doubt. But also, at a crucial moment, when the shift supervisor lost his temper at me, I'd been able to keep ahold of mine. The way this all happened seemed nothing short of a major miracle.

CHAPTER NINE

The SGI works locally, nationally and worldwide in 192 countries and territories to promote peace, culture and education. I worked wholeheartedly as a young women's leader in my SGI community where I felt needed and appreciated. (Our leaders in cities, towns and rural areas around the globe are all volunteers. And due to the egalitarian nature of this Buddhism, whether one has a leadership position or not, if one chants and takes action for the happiness of others, that person is a leader too.)

One day, several of us got together at a member's home to plan an upcoming discussion meeting. I always marveled at the china dolls and all the antique baby dolls decorating the black-lacquered curio cabinets in her living room. Although the other three sat on the floor with their legs folded under them, a position I never could master, I chose the couch for comfort.

We finished chanting and reciting short excerpts from the Lotus Sutra, and then silently offered prayers of gratitude, prayers for world peace, for the continuation of our own profound inner transformation, for the fulfillment of all our wishes, for the deceased, and for the happiness of all living beings. Then we began to plan.

"Daniel and I got together to study last week," I shared. "He enjoys learning about this practice as much as I do. His mom's still pretty sick, though. On oxygen all day long now. But I think Daniel might like to share an experience at our next discussion meeting. What do you think, Susan?" Daniel was a friend of Susan's whom she had introduced to the practice. "You want to call and ask him?"

I looked at the woman moderating the meeting. Susan was a no-nonsense type. Capable of organizing the local initiative for the Million Man March on Washington, D.C., Susan carried a strong sense of responsibility for the success of our peace movement and the happiness of our members. I'd learned a lot from her, and she often encouraged me to take the initiative and get creative in our meetings.

"You know, you shouldn't be visiting young men like that," Susan said crossly. Her corn rows tied in a clump behind her head and dark brown freckles on her light chocolate cheeks, she held a pen and piece of paper ready to write down our plans.

"Why? Daniel and I are friends," I said, surprised by her tone.

"It just isn't proper."

"Well, I don't agree. We have fun studying together, and his mom loves it when I come over and visit with her."

"Let's move on to plan the meeting," Susan said abruptly.

Everyone thought for a minute.

"How 'bout we start with a song this time?" I suggested. I often performed songs or led the group in singing.

"No, I don't think so." Susan objected.

"But, why not?"

"Kathy, why do you always have to cause problems?"

There it was. My stepmother's tone.

I often felt inferior to this woman and afraid to express myself about personal matters. Now, my anxiety was taking over. "Wait a minute." I stood up from the couch and took a step towards her. My heart beating hard, fear heightened, I asked, "Why are you being this way?"

She jumped to her feet. Without our shoes on we stood eye to eye. Until that moment, I always thought she was a lot taller than me.

"You know you should never get in some-one's face like that, towering over me while I'm sitting on the floor. Don't you have any respect?!" she shouted.

I felt as if a snake were spitting out venom at me. Dumbly, not knowing what to do, I reached over with two fingers to touch her shoulder. I hoped this move would calm her down and somehow penetrate the barrier between us. It didn't.

In a flash, Susan knocked my hand away brusquely as if it were a detested thing. Before I knew it, we were rolling on the floor. Hands grabbing arms, pushing and pulling, feet kicking legs.

Then, I felt hands behind me, on my shoulders, gently pulling me away. The other two members helped separate us. The maelstrom over, I began to tremble uncontrollably and weep.

"If you weren't a member, I'd call the police on you!" Susan yelled just before she stormed out of the house.

I stayed behind and talked with the others. What had just happened? I couldn't fathom it. None of us could.

Mortified, I wrote letter after letter to Susan in my journal—not to send her, but to get my thoughts straight, to practice taking responsibility and get to the truth of it all. I chanted for her happiness and to appreciate her Buddha nature. How had things gotten so out of control? I knew I'd been traumatized umpteen times. Had I just flipped out?

As she and I had rolled around on the floor, I recall feeling like it represented a battle between me and my step-mother and even others who had hurt me so badly. But, of course, she wasn't any of those people. She was just a person with karma of her own to work through and change. And a catalyst helping me recognize some deeply entrenched trauma so I could work towards healing from it. She wasn't the "bad guy" here. But neither was I. Neither of us had meant to hurt the other.

More than a month went by, and Susan hadn't responded to my phone calls. Some of our area's senior leaders agreed to help me arrange a discussion between the two of us. I was eager to own up to my responsibility for our fight and to work on some understanding between us, some empathy towards each other, some closure for us both. It seemed natural that Susan would want to do some owning up too. But that's not what happened.

After I apologized and expressed remorse, Susan simply said, "Well, I don't blame Kathy for what happened. I blame it all on her bipolar disorder."

I was stunned. I didn't know what to say. I knew it was way beyond that. But my inability to communicate effectively and my sense of inferiority around Susan and the rest of the people in the room prevented me from thinking clearly or speaking my truth. I wished I could've explained how, whenever I picked up the phone, I never knew whether Susan would be in a good mood or bad, whether she'd treat me with kindness and appreciation, which she often did, or startle me with anger and disapproval. Or explain how I felt as a young person—that the middle-aged Susan seemed condescending, like she was always in the driver's seat, always knew best.

I'd gone to a dangerous crack neighbor-hood where Susan's daughter lived in a broken-down shack with her crack-dealing boyfriend to let her know one of her peers cared. I reached out in the hopes of saving her daughter from more suffering, to show her how important her life was. I would do anything to help Susan and her daughter. But then I could never establish boundaries with Susan or explain that her short temper and angry tone of voice intimidated me and made me feel small.

I was certain the fight had little to do with the irritability of bipolar disorder. I'd been on medication for years by then and rarely exper-ienced anger—depression, numbness and fear, yes, but little anger. Rather, I believe it resulted from the buttons of my deep-seated inferiority complex and post traumatic stress disorder (PTSD) getting pushed over and over again in conversations with Susan. That day, I'd finally gone over the edge. I'd actually lost consciousness from the time she pushed my arm to the moments we were rolling around on the floor. But I was the one who'd been triggered. Although I don't remember it, I'm sure I grabbed her first.

After this, hostilities broke out between another friend and me; with a young African-American woman who, like me, had chosen to take responsibility in our sangha to support other youth. We'd done some great work together for quite a while, but after the fight with Susan, she and I had a terrible argument. I don't remember raging at her, but her responsive epithet made it clear I had. Since the altercation, it seemed a black box like Pandora's had been opened, and at times I could garner little self-control over those negative functions stemming from my fundamental darkness.

Perhaps due, in part, to these circumstances, the book *The Color Purple* captivated me. It deepened my sense of empathy for people of color.

It so happens that Tina Turner is a member of SGI-USA. Watching the movie about her life, *What's Love Got to Do With It?*, gave me a clue to at least one of the major issues I needed help with. Standing in the theatre surrounded by strangers, I yelled at the movie screen during the scene when her then-husband rapes her. It was undeniable. The psychological wounds from the sexual assault were a gaping maw, and I desperately needed help.

As damaging as the violence between Susan and me was, I'm grateful that it helped me recognize my PTSD, so I could start seeking the help I needed to begin the healing process. Until then, I'd been somewhat oblivious.

I knew the group's compassionate energy was behind Susan and me, too, to help us both transform this and grow. The day actually came, years later, when Susan acknowledged how arrogant she'd been at the time, and we were able to speak as friends again. In this admission, she shared responsibility, and that was *big*.

For that, I remain extremely grateful, and I

suspect Susan had a charitable reason for originally blaming the bipolar disorder when all this went down. It wasn't only to spare herself embarrassment but also to spare me. She didn't know I was suffering from PTSD nor about any of my traumas. So perhaps in her mind she thought that if people believed it all happened due to my bipolar disorder, that I couldn't help myself, then I wouldn't be judged so harshly for my actions.

I'm also grateful that this experience set me on a path to transforming the tendency for arrogance that I also had, the other side of the coin from the insecurity and cowardice I easily identified in myself. That way I could become someone able to embrace all kinds of people with egalitarianism, courage, confidence, warmth, and humility.

But in the aftermath of our fight, I simply felt alienated from everyone, including myself. My feelings confused me. I didn't understand them nor the reactions I had to people and their reactions to me. I felt developmentally disabled, extremely immature, unable to connect with people on so many levels. Things spiraled downward. I made misguided choices in friends, and they convinced me to write junk about someone we knew for a slanderous magazine. I experienced backlash from people about that and became more and more rageful. The therapist I'd been working with for almost a year was shocked and a little frightened when I screamed in rage at him during a session.

I journaled a lot, trying to understand people, my shortcomings and strengths, and why I couldn't grow up. And to try to discern the hopeful, positive side of things. But then, I screamed at a dear friend in public during a game of putt-putt golf. I said it was for his own good. But he refused to talk with me after that. Said I'd lost his trust. The loss of this friend tore at my heart more than losing a friend ever had before.

I fell into a dark depression. My behavior at work indicated a problem when I had the only argument with a staff member I'd ever had at the hospital in the four years I'd worked there. I was put on probation.

Within a year of the fight with Susan, I entered a psychiatric unit again. It was a short stay though. Medication adjustment. Seven days. No counseling.

When I got back to work, shift supervisor Tom, whom I dearly respected, shared some distressing "insider" information with me. "Kathy, I hate to tell you this. And I know it's going to be hard to hear, but I think it's better you know rather than being in the dark. It came up in one of our supervisor staff meetings that the fact that you have bipolar disorder completely disqualifies you from ever 'moving up the ladder' in the hospital."

"What? How can they do that?"

"I didn't have any part in this decision. And frankly, I don't think it was right that we sat there openly discussing your diagnosis like that. It's supposed to be confidential. So I felt I should tell you, that you had a right to know."

How embarrassing. I'd told Tom about my disorder late the previous year, shortly after he became my supervisor. And after the fight between Susan and me, I needed to explain my bipolar to my department head because a severe depression had prevented me from being able to call into work for a couple days. But how could my department head allow discussion of my disorder like that at a hospital staff meeting? Not to mention deciding I wasn't promotion material because of it. I really couldn't escape the feeling of humiliation and betrayal.

And what could I do? Nothing, I thought. What was my karmic tendency? Since the altercation with Susan, I had regressed so much. I was back to seeing myself as a victim: helpless, powerless, and hopeless. Within a month, depression prevented me from leaving my apartment. I didn't know my illness probably qualified me for medical disability insurance that I'd paid into at work. I didn't know I could have reported my company for ethics violations. I just sank into my old beat-up twin mattress that laid on the floor of my tiny efficiency apartment and stayed there nearly all day every day. I attempted a return to work, but within a week my heart began feeling like it was being put through a meat grinder every time I went into the department. After two months of living off my savings, on the day I should've been celebrating my thirty-fifth birthday, I quit my job. I was just six months shy of my fifth anniversary at the hospital.

CHAPTER TEN

Fortunately, around that time, my close friend JT needed my help. We'd met at an SGI youth activity in late 1996. He worked at the same hospital I did, but as a technician on the psychiatric unit. His presence there had helped me feel safe on the unit when I'd been admitted in mid-1998 before I quit the hospital that November.

JT had been the friend on the receiving end of my rage at the putt-putt golf place some months after the fight with Susan, but he had chosen to forgive me a few months after that. Perhaps he sensed that I was determined, no matter what, to be a much better friend. It's because JT had shut me out that I did my practice with all-out earnestness to become truly compassionate and win back his friendship.

At one point as I chanted for JT's happiness, I felt lifted free of all the walls around my heart, as if this were how a newborn baby must feel. Early on in my practice, I had experienced feelings of expansion, the opposite of the shrinking feelings I'd had as a child. Those were cool and enjoyable, for sure. But now, for the first time, I was experiencing the sensitive vulnerability and sublime nature of the human heart—free, open, light, and delighted. I awoke the next morning feeling the same, like my skin was brand new and gravity no longer held me down.

A phone call from Susan changed that though. We hadn't spoken in a while except at meetings. She was in one of her moods again.

"Kathy, are you going on the trip to the Florida Nature and Culture Center next Saturday?" The FNCC conference center, located in Ft. Lauderdale, is a beautiful gift President Ikeda gave to the members. We sometimes took day trips to activities there. "You need to let me know, so I can reserve your seat on the bus."

Now, she could have said this in a sweet way, or even with simple courtesy like it was a business transaction. But that wasn't the mood Susan was in that morning. Instead, she sounded accusatory, like I'd purposely refrained from calling her about this just so she'd have a bad day.

Now normally I could brace myself for her sharpness, but due to my current spiritual experience, my defenses were down so that her words felt like a switchblade stabbing me in the chest.

I answered in the affirmative. "Yes. I want to go."

But then she had more to say to me, all in her angry tone, and all I wanted to do was stop feeling her shrill voice.

Finally, I thought of the words I needed to end the conversation. "Susan, I've got to go. Bye."

I hung up the phone, grabbing my pillow to muffle my screams so my house landlords on the other side of the wall couldn't hear. Until that moment, I'd never known the full extent of the rage, pain, and fear seething like molten lava in the darkness of my life.

As if my environment were reflecting the intensity of the emotional energy I expelled into my pillow, a lion escaped from a nearby zoo that same day. Until that day, Susan never seemed to get it, that her angry words literally hurt me. But with the awareness that we're all connected, I felt certain my outcry had touched her somehow, and I chanted to be sure some good came of it. Sure enough, that was the very last time Susan ever addressed me angrily. Through the energetic airwaves of the heart, her heart finally got the message.

This experience also taught me how intense was the suffering I must've caused JT when I raged at him at the putt-putt golf place. I was only just beginning to perceive the profound sensitivity of the human heart.

Life teaches hard lessons sometimes. After I screamed into my pillow with rage, I was no longer able to feel free and light. But something a friend said soon after this assured me that my practice, hospital job and supporting others was all helping me change inside in a big way.

The friend was Terry. He'd moved out of state years before, and we hadn't seen each other since then. He came back to finalize some things with his ex-wife and visited friends while here. He and I wound up hanging out fishing at the beach.

Witnessing my life condition, after all that time apart, struck him. At dinner that evening he said, "Kathy, I can hardly believe how much you've changed since I last saw you. You exude such a gentle radiance that it's like I'm talking to a different person. Not at all like you were as a cab driver."

"Wow, Terry. With what I've been going through this past year, that's something I really needed to hear. Thank you."

The best dinner I'd ever had transpired that night.

So, now, I didn't have a job, was too depressed to look for one, and had to live off my savings, but JT needed me. At a time when I was down the most, I could at least help my precious friend. Efforts for his sake helped me feel like I had something worthwhile to do to help me keep moving forward, even if just a little.

JT called me. He had forgiven me about six months earlier when we talked during my inpatient stay. "Hi, Kathy. I just got released from the hospital and thought to call you."

"What? Why were you in the hospital?" I heard agitation in his voice.

"They Baker Acted me!"[6]

"What? Who did?"

"The hospital."

"Why in the world did our employer have you committed to a psych ward against your will?"

"Well, it's a little complicated."

"Oh. Okay." I waited for him to go on.

"About a month ago, we had a sociopath on the psych ward. He hadn't been screened thoroughly yet, and we didn't know what he was capable of. Well, he wound up breaking into the nurse's station. And when he broke down the door, he knocked my friend Ken, another tech on the ward, unconscious. Ken was in a coma for about a week. But then he died."

"Oh, my God, JT!"

"I stayed with him until the end. He and I had been really close friends. And after he died, I got so damn mad! It should have never happened!"

"What did you do?"

"After Ken passed, my supervisors and the hospital administrator called in all of the staff involved for a meeting about the incident. I stood up and told our department chief what I thought. I said that a sociopath shouldn't have been on our unit. He should have been screened properly, so he wasn't on our unit in the first place. But, in the event someone like that gets overlooked, the problem could've been prevented if we'd had more than one security guard on the unit. Ken died because of penny-pinching!"

He paused for a minute. I didn't say anything.

"Before the incident, we'd approached the head of our department and the hospital administration over and over about the lax security situation. But they refused to let us have more than one guard for our whole unit."

He paused. I waited. What could I possibly say to him? There was no way to ameliorate his pain.

"Oh, JT. I'm so sorry about your friend."

"Thanks."

"But I still don't understand why you were Baker Acted?"

"In the meeting, they told me I needed to calm down," he continued. "They seemed to think something was wrong with me because I was so upset. I certainly wasn't going to calm down at their insistence. So I left. On the way to my car, two hospital security police stopped me. They said they were concerned about me. That I should go with them. They made it clear I didn't have any choice in the matter. They turned me over to two Orlando police officers who took me to the little hospital in Longwood and forced me into an involuntary admission."

"How could they get away with that?"

"I don't know. But they did. They kept me there for seventy-two hours, trying to force medication on me. I'm so pissed off about it!"

"Gosh, JT. It's so hard to believe this happened to you."

We both thought a moment.

I said, "I mean, you know I've been mistreated in psych wards before. But you're so together. You *work* in the mental health field. How could they have done that to you?!"

"Well, they did."

I paused for his anger to subside.

"So, I'm gonna be on workers' comp for a while," he continued. "That gives me time to work on the lawsuit I'm filing against them. Then I thought of you. I know how good you are at writing. Will you help me write up my grievance?"

He knew what my answer would be before he even asked.

Though still depressed myself, I now had something important to do. And what better friend to help than JT? I'd learned a lot about the meaning of compassion from him in the two years we'd known each other. I would never forget the night he called me not long after the fight between Susan and me. I had been crying a lot for many nights, so hard sometimes that I felt my guts would burst. On that night he called and asked me how I was doing. I was too embarrassed to confide in him or even let him know I was upset. I only swallowed my sobs, so he wouldn't hear me. But I couldn't hide it completely. He knew I was suffering, but he wisely didn't try to pry.

Instead, he told me about the monkeys he was watching on a public television show. As he described the monkeys and what they were doing, I began to laugh at the visions of monkeys I saw in my mind's eye. By the time he finished, I had stitches in my sides, and my sorrows had vanished. His Bodhisattva spirit shone its brightest in my life that night. I looked forward to helping him now.

"Sure, JT. You know I'll help. And anyway, I've got time on my hands now, too, since I've just quit my job at the hospital."

"Oh, Kathy, I didn't know."

"Yeah. Well, it was coming. I needed a change anyway." No sense piling my worries onto him at this point.

For weeks, we worked side by side on my computer.

Once we finished, he told me he was moving away. "Yeah, I'm gonna go visit my father up North. I haven't seen him in a few years, and he's ill."

"I'm glad you're going to go see your dad. But I'll miss you." I paused. "I know you're still really angry about what happened, JT. About your friend and the injustice of it all. I know how it is to feel angry like that. But remember how we use our Buddhist practice to "change poison into medicine?" I really believe you'll be able to use this anger of yours to change something for the better. And the anger you're feeling now really won't last forever."

"Thanks for telling me that, Kathy. It's something I needed to hear. And I think you're right."

CHAPTER ELEVEN

At a state employment agency, I was encouraged to apply for unemployment insurance. Finding I was eligible, I decided to return to school for my Bachelor's degree in Communications. I already had earned my AA degree during my last year at the hospital, and there was nothing I needed more desperately than to learn better communication skills and actualize this most basic process of human interaction. I moved out of my "hermitage" studio efficiency to share an apartment close to the university.

Before school started that fall in 1999, during the Labor Day holiday, I flew to Iowa for a family reunion to celebrate my grandfather's ninetieth birthday. Mom and I shared both a hotel room and our insatiable desire for snack food. We raided the motel vending machines every night, something I was secretly ashamed of.

It had been years since Mom and I had spent any time together. In that close proximity, it was no surprise we had our disagreements. But one night our mild clashes escalated. I stood at the door ready to storm out of the room and turned to look at her as she ate potato chips. Something welled up in me, and I raged at her at the top of my lungs, "Why didn't you ever write me when I was little? I know you were hospitalized a lot and struggled with alcoholism, but you never even called me or Brian. For years!! You left me there in Margaret's house. Then you took us back for a year but didn't keep us. That made things even worse when we had to go back to living with Dad and Margaret. Do you know how much I cried every night for you when I was little? What kind of a mother doesn't call or write her kids for years? How could you *do* that!"

Mom just sat on her bed like a deer in the headlights, reeling from the venom I spewed out at her with the intensity of a hurricane. Neither of us saw that coming. Ever since I became old enough to be told that she'd been hospitalized at Cherokee multiple times, received electroconvulsive shock therapy to bring her out of her catatonic depressions (which Mom's mother said dramatically altered her personality), and lost herself in the bottle for years both before and after she attempted suicide, in my head I never blamed her. I knew manic-depression had a lot to do with why she couldn't stay in contact with us.

But obviously the hurt child in me didn't understand and had never gotten over it. All my hurt shot out at her that night.

Prior to the Labor Day weekend family reunion, in April of that year, the Columbine shootings happened at a high school in Colorado. The two teenage shooters committed suicide afterwards. In immediate response to this crisis, youth in the SGI-USA took action in local communities and regions all across the nation in what our national youth leaders named the Victory Over Violence (VOV) campaign. VOV continues to educate about and help transform the tendency to disrespect one's own life and the lives of others that leads to violence, passive violence, and the apathy or helplessness that turns a blind eye and accepts violence as necessary or unavoidable. I proudly participated in the movement that summer.

I didn't know then that Mom was violently abused in childhood. And now, in that hotel room, with the verbal violence of a screaming rampage, I'd just disrespected the woman who'd given birth to me. I couldn't take it back. I couldn't apologize it away. And I didn't know her feelings would be so deeply affected for so long afterwards.

One of the most basic tenets of the wonderful philosophy I practice is to become the kind of person who respects her parents. Especially one's mother. Thirteenth-century Buddhist reformer, Nichiren Daishonin, who established this Buddhist practice for the empowerment of the common people, actually asserted in male-dominated Japan that men and women were equal. In his writings is the passage, "Hell is in the heart of a person who inwardly despises his father and disregards his mother."[7] And in a letter to one of his closest friends, he wrote, "More valuable than treasures in a storehouse are the treasures of the body, and the treasures of the heart are the most valuable of all. From the time you read this letter on, strive to accumulate the treasures of the heart!"[8]

How long would it take me to demonstrate these treasures of the heart?[9] I apologized to Mom with deep sincerity before the end of the reunion, and she never took issue with me. She just let it drop. Never defended herself or criticized me. Years later, when she spoke to me apologetically about how she hadn't been there for us as kids, I sensed she had internalized some deep shame since I'd fileted her with my knifelike criticisms. What kind of awful daughter loses her temper like that? What had possessed me? How would I ever make it up to her?

After the reunion and my verbal assault on Mom, I sunk into the deepest hole. A totally incapacitating depression. (I didn't realize until years later that my attack of rage and the excessive guilt that followed led to this depressive episode.) I had to withdraw from all my classes. I slept on the floor and could hardly leave my bedroom.

One might think Susan would choose to distance herself from me after the problems between us, especially with my moods and temper becoming more severe, but she didn't. Susan worried so much about me that she brought a warm and insightful friend of hers to visit me, a person rich with experiences of winning with the one essential phrase. Her friend said I needed to become strong and encouraged me to use my spiritual practice for that purpose. I felt lighter after they left, and I saw Susan in a very different light from then on too.

But as much as I agreed with them in

principle, becoming strong in reality seemed impossible at the time; having stronger self-control a truly impossible dream. As things were, I acted insecure, paranoid, anxious, and impatient around my three roommates. One of them began looking at me with fear in her eyes whenever we came into contact with each other. Another avoided me. The third and I began arguing. She seemed to have anger issues all her own but never let her tongue loose unless we were alone. Lucky me!

She'd come to my bedroom and scream things through the door at me when everyone else was out. Only I seemed to warrant her rageful tirades. Talk about karma. I was getting what I deserved though. What I put out into the universe, I attracted. But with such a temper, didn't that roommate need to be on medication herself? I felt sure of it.

My theory went unproven, however. One day I was called to the apartment manager's office. My roommates had filed a complaint. I would be evicted unless I left of my own accord. I chose the latter.

CHAPTER TWELVE

Before that happened, I'd already returned to school part time for the spring semester, begun attending various Twelve Step meetings to see how a recovery program could help me make sense of my compulsive eating disorder, and started my personal communication training in earnest. In these meetings, I learned to train my mind to listen to and learn from others' experiences. I also felt empowered and supported to share my honest feelings as others listened to and learned from me. Alongside my Buddhist practice, this therapeutic group experience along with compassionate one-to-one peer work and professional counseling began teaching me how to communicate more effectively and ask for help and support, how to better navigate human relationships and stop isolating. All this helped me start healing. It dramatically altered my two-dimensional perceptions of life and relationships created by many years of learning from the two-dimensional medium of television ever since I was an isolated kid.

In fact, during my first few years of being in the recovery rooms for my food addiction, in an early morning Twelve Step meeting for people struggling with alcohol, among about one hundred participants, I was able to feel and express the terror I'd carried from my last four-point restraint experience. The monster's vice-like pincers were no longer suffocating me, and I sobbed and trembled uncontrollably among my peers. Then the most surprising thing happened. Compassionate responses from men I didn't know personally who'd experienced something similar melted my heart. This healing experience assured me for the first time in my life that there were men with caring hearts in the world at large in addition to the male SGI leaders and friends who'd long sup-ported, encouraged and guided me through the years. My trust in men grew.

Another powerful healing experience took place in a therapy session. Sometime after my terror had been addressed, this session helped me get in touch with the anger and resentment towards those who'd tied me down. Holding my male therapist's hands in a way that would not hurt him, I was able to feel and share that anger with someone else by squeezing his hands with every ounce of my strength. I let out my rage about the abuse both verbally and physically so I was no longer carrying it alone. I could start to let it go completely.

These experiences took place a while after my roommate troubles. But immediately before being forced out of that shared apartment, despite my emotional turmoil and problems getting along with people, I managed to start doing some good in my new job. The college granted me a part-time, work-study assignment tutoring elementary school kids who had trouble learning to read. I went so far as to explain my embarrassing trespassing misdemeanor some fifteen years before in order to clear the background check. I would do anything for this assignment. In a temp job supervising children the previous summer, I realized there was a population of people I not only got along with easily but actually enjoyed being around. This, in itself, was evidence of a big change in karma considering all the years I was convinced kids were afraid of me like I was of them.

Some of the children I tutored had ADD or ADHD or attended a special education classroom part of the school day. For the first time, I saw I had a knack for something, and these tutoring sessions felt like nirvana experiences. No, I hadn't gone off my medications and become manic. It wasn't a high. It was a joy that I can only describe as like looking in the mirror and feeling I had entered another dimension.

Kids became my favorite people to learn from after that. I've worked with children and side-by-side with young people a lot in the SGI, and doing so has always been a boost to my morale. Their openness and idealism makes them easier for me to trust. And given the right tools, they'll exceed one's wildest expectations in achieving what might seem totally impossible.

Just a few short years ago, I joined with over 30,000 youth in SGI-USA in the Rock the Era Youth Culture Festival. Our aim? To accept the "baton" from our mentor to achieve world peace, (referred to in Japanese as kosen-rufu), united as one in our resolve to accomplish this noble, albeit *seemingly* impossible, dream.

According to www.ploughshares.org, as of 2015 there were 15,695 nuclear warheads world-wide. But in response to the call for nuclear abolition to 50,000 youth in 1957 by Japanese educator and second Soka Gakkai president,

Josei Toda—imprisoned and persecuted during World War II because he wouldn't change his religious beliefs to support the Japanese military government's war efforts—more and more students and youth across America and the world are joining to educate each other and the public in one-to-one dialogues about the very real and ever-present threat of nuclear annihilation. The SGI is determinedly promoting the philosophy of the sanctity of life, and in cooperation with other organizations, is creating greater awareness of the need to outlaw such weapons for the basic security of the human race.

Since 1957, university founder, children's book author, and International Poet of Peace award recipient, SGI President Ikeda, among many other things, has spearheaded the SGI's nuclear abolition movement as President Toda's direct successor. In the introduction to his historical novel, *The New Human Revolution*, Dr. Ikeda writes: "Mahatma Gandhi proclaimed that the 'power of the spirit' is stronger than any atomic bomb. To transform this century of war into a century of peace, we must cultivate the limitless inherent power of human life. This is the 'human revolution'..."[10, 11]

Great teachers and students throughout history have demonstrated time and time again that the influence of a single individual can change the course of history. How powerful it must be, then, when thousands and even millions of awakened citizens join in such an endeavor. Look at the Arab Spring of 2011 and the Million Man March on Washington, DC. The world has witnessed dictators being overthrown by nonviolence and an African-American in the White House because of the strength and unity of the common people.

And isn't our culture beginning to recognize more and more that, to become a great individual, one needs a great teacher or mentor in life? Some people have that in a parent, grandparent, schoolteacher, coach, a great philosopher from history, or someone else who showed with their lives how to become a great human being.

As for me, remember the old TV show *Kung Fu* in which David Carradine plays the peace-loving, Shaolin monk who walks across America righting wrongs with the help of his expertise in martial-arts? In every episode, he has a flashback of some lesson that he learned from his teacher that reminds him of how to act with integrity and effectively transform his current situation for the better—for everyone. Ever since watching that TV series as a kid, I began wishing for my own great teacher. Some altruistic friend who cares for your well-being more than you do yourself, who believes in you more than you believe in yourself, and even knows you better than you know yourself. Someone who demonstrates, with every action, a correct way of life and teaches, by example, how to become strong and victorious rather than be thrown off course by life's vicissitudes.

Dr. Ikeda also writes: "A Buddha holds others in the highest regard. Kosen-rufu[12] means promulgating this attitude of respect for human beings."[13]

That's how I felt when I met my great mentor, a person who has been compared with such outstanding human rights leaders as Mahatma Gandhi and Dr. Martin Luther King, Jr.[14] When I met my mentor, Professor Ikeda, who has fought tirelessly behind the scenes in the global community as an ordinary citizen for world peace and the happiness of others for nearly seventy years, he looked into my eyes as if he saw in me the most important person on the planet. His spirit of profound respect for me penetrated the walls of self-loathing around my heart, communicating the vital importance of the work only I could do in the world. Learning from such a mentor is truly a most wonderful and precious thing.

Something told me being a classroom teacher was not the right kind of work for me, and I wasn't allowed to keep tutoring as a work-study student if I wasn't an education major. So by my final year in college, I'd changed jobs. Working with children and teens part time as a behavioral technician really tore up my nerves though. Storms of anxiety swirled in my heart during every session. My first grader had tantrums on the floor of his classroom. A second grader had a tendency to lie. Then the doctors placed my first grader on psychiatric medication. My heart broke for him. He seemed so lost, beaten, and listless. Then I lost my temper with the teenager I worked with. I shouted at her for some bad behavior. That should have been my first clue that being off my psychiatric medication was a bad idea.

I had stopped taking them some months

before 9/11 happened. Then, like many people, depression took hold after I kept seeing the images of the planes hitting the twin towers. Unable to leave my bed for days at a time, I couldn't attend classes regularly. But I didn't want to withdraw. I was so close to graduating.

So, I "sucked it up," as they say, to finish my last two semesters, and I became an intermittent high achiever. That means I'd use the manic upswings in my cycle to hurry and catch up on my school work with an urgency to compensate for those times when I couldn't function in the low end of the cycle.

I also established a student club on campus called Students for a Culture of Peace that held Buddhist philosophy discussion meetings. It wasn't easy since I had to write up our lengthy club constitution from scratch and gather the required number of signatures of students willing to be a part of the club. With that, on top of my classes and stressful job, anxiety reigned supreme in my last semester during the finishing touches and first couple preparatory meetings of the club. Then, our club sponsor, the dean of religious studies, had his own ideas for the club. When our visions didn't mesh, the club almost didn't materialize. He was also battling cancer and seemed ready to pull out of sponsoring us.

Around this crucial time, when it seemed the club wouldn't make it, an elderly SGI member, a lady I had admired, passed away. She was loved by many, and her death hit me very hard. I'd visited her several times, and even though near the end she was often unconscious, I still reported to her and her husband at her hospital bedside how things were shaping up for the club. I knew how excited she had been about it. Then, after she passed away, in my most extreme moment of worry, insecurity and doubt about the club and my capabilities, I felt her presence, like she was there with me.

It was as if she was cheering me on, telling me, "Don't give up. You can do this. You're almost there."

And I had hope again. The original sponsoring professor helped us get a new sponsor. Our new club became official.

CHAPTER THIRTEEN

But then, the journalist Danny Pearl was executed by terrorists. I remember my shock, horror, and rage—screaming at the top of my lungs as I drove my car, almost veering off of the interstate. His wife is a member of SGI-France. His murder felt very personal.

That same week, hypomanic me told a guy I liked my entire life story in the span of an evening. How could I ruin our chances at a relationship like that? *Stupid me*, I thought. No, unmedicated, soon-to-be hyp*er*manic me. I stayed awake for ten days, except for dozing off a few times for fifteen or twenty minutes.

At the downtown Orlando Crisis Stabilization Unit, at just after midnight, I rang the buzzer and talked to a technician through the window. "I think I'm the reincarnation of Jesus or Mary Magdalene or the Virgin Mary." Heck, maybe I was even the reincarnation of Shakyamuni Buddha. But I didn't say that. "I haven't slept for ten days. Can I stay here?"

"Do you have insurance?"

"Yes."

"You don't want to stay here. This is where drunks and drug addicts come to get clean. It's pretty rough. Why don't you try one of the hospitals?"

Feeling I wasn't safe, I drove away anxiously. No way was I going to the same hospital where JT and I had worked after what they did to us. I drove to the only other hospital I could think of.

On the way, I stopped at a green light for some reason. All of a sudden, a huge utility truck barreled across the intersection in front of me, right through a red light. And I thought, *Wow, I'm in danger more than I realized*, thankful for pausing when I did.

I hadn't been in this hospital's emergency room. I told the nurse the same thing I'd told the technician at the Orlando CSU. She checked my vitals and directed me to the waiting room. As I waited, I could have sworn a cartoon pixie on the TV was showing me a special gateway into heaven. A secret between me and the TV people.

I went into the sparsely populated children's waiting room and laid down on my back on a short, round, yellow table. No children were present at the time. I envisioned my spirit was like Godzilla, stomping on the hospital that had done my friend JT and me wrong. *This will teach them*, I thought, as I stomped my feet on the floor and banged the back of my upper arms and elbows against the table.

Eventually called into the back to be examined, I waited on a gurney behind a curtain. I noticed that when I bent my neck backwards off the head of the little bed on wheels and pointed the top of my head towards the floor, I felt calmer and somehow reassured. It would be years before I understood why this action affected me that way.

An intern came in to interview me. As he sat down next to me I said, "I haven't slept for ten days, and I'm having delusions or hallucinations or something. I think I need to be admitted to the psych unit."

He said little and left the room. He returned shortly with a prescription. "Here. Take this to an all-night pharmacy. It's a script for several doses of sleep medication. That'll help."

I looked at the script and saw they were a lightweight medication. I doubted they'd get me to sleep. "Really? You don't think it's that serious or that I should be admitted?" I asked.

"Well, I spoke with the chief resident. I told him your concerns. He said you should be fine with one good night's sleep."

I stared at him in disbelief. "Okay." And I took the prescription. Again, I didn't feel safe, but I wasn't the doctor. What could I do? Oh, I could've made a scene. But that could lead to another visit to a seclusion room. And I was too lost and enervated to be rageful anyway.

I couldn't get my car started and asked a guy for a jumpstart. It worked, and I drove from the hospital parking area to the traffic light to turn on to the main road. All of a sudden, I noticed a beautiful ray of light streaming down in the middle of the intersection. The traffic light was red. I opened my car door to step out and go into the ray of light. I was sure Jesus was calling me up into heaven and the light would take me there.

The car behind me honked just then. Rain poured in on me, and the sound startled me. I got back in my car and drove to the all-night pharmacy.

When I got home, I forgot about the pills. Some winter Olympic Games were happening on TV. The cheers and accolades, all the smiles and applause, were for me, weren't they? My psychotic delusions had full control over my mind by then, and the whole world was cheering me on. Something was wrong with this picture. I turned the channel to an old movie.

I sat at my computer and read an email a friend had just written me. She lived in Tennessee. I'd recently emailed her a personal update.

"Kathy, I'm worried about you. Are you taking your medication?"

My last message must've been really out there. I didn't reply.

But the one thing on my mind was, *It's definitely time for the Second Coming of Christ. I feel it. I know it.* I hadn't gone to church in years.

I respected many Christians I knew and the good works they'd done, but that hadn't been my faith for a long time. Still I thought, *I'd better make sure I'm following all the commandments, or I won't get to ride up to heaven during the Second Coming. It's gonna happen any day now.* My thoughts raced through the ten commandments, anxiety high.

Oh, no! My heart froze. *I'm going to be left behind because of this!* I looked towards my altar where I did my practice and thought, *I've got to get rid of it!*

Then I did something so unspeakably destructive I cannot write about it at this point. But I can share the effect of what I did. Years before this, I accidentally broke a large mirror in the locker room at Sea World before I quit my job there. Ever since then, the superstitious part of me would reflect on how bad my life had become after that. I had definitely had seven years of bad luck.

Standing in my apartment that night, realizing what I'd just done, I felt certain I'd be cursed for as long as if I'd just broken ten thousand mirrors. No doubt, I'd be walking through hell on earth for the rest of my life.

I've got to get a gun and shoot myself in the head! I said aloud to no one. Frantic, I reconsidered. *No, let me call Ann. She'll know what to do. She'll help.*

Ann was a good friend who is a senior in faith in our sangha. She lived only five minutes from my house. But each time I called, the phone kept making loud, grinding beeps like it was out of order.

Shit! Damn! I tried to think. *Okay, let me drive there.* My heart was thumping fast. *But what if my car won't start again like what happened at the hospital? Nobody's going to give me a jump at three o'clock in the morning.* Frantically, I ran down the stairs to my car.

The car did start up, and I made it to Ann's. I told her what I'd done. She took me back home and helped me find one of the heavily sedating anti-psychotic medications in my kitchen cupboard that always got me to sleep— something my disordered mind had forgotten about for those entire ten days.

"We'd better call the hospital to get you admitted."

"Yeah," I agreed.

And so, we did.

CHAPTER FOURTEEN

It only took me a week to get out of the hospital and back on my feet, thanks in large part to doing my practice on the psych unit. I promised Ann I'd stay on my anti-psychotic medication after that. To never go off it again without consulting my doctor.

It was my last semester, and I had a lot of studying to do for midterms and papers due. But the new heavily sedating anti-psychotic Zyprexa improved my concentration a lot. (It'd be years before I discovered its debilitating health effects.) So I thought only of my school work and not about those ten thousand broken mirrors.

My boss, AJ, the one who had trained me the previous fall as a behavior technician, had seen something special in me from the get go. I sensed he believed in me more than any boss ever had. He even suggested I take the training to be a behavior analyst, so I could make good money in this kind of altruistic career path. But after I was released from the hospital, he called me into his office.

"Did you miss some sessions with clients and not call into the office about it?"

"Um, yes AJ. I've been really having some medical problems. I'm sorry I let you and the clients down."

"I'm sorry too, Kathy. I really liked having you work here and, initially, I received great reports about the work you were doing. But, as it is, we can't afford to have any of our technicians miss sessions like that. The clients will suffer. I hope you understand."

"Yes, I do."

I was actually going to be free of a job that put my heart into a blender turned on high, and I could concentrate on my finals. That was okay with me. All except for one thing: I had let AJ down.

"You can write up a formal letter of resignation."

I sensed he wanted me to be able to leave with at least a semblance of dignity *and* not have a termination on my employment record.

"Thanks, AJ. I appreciate it. You've really been the best boss I've ever had. Thank you for believing in me. I wish things could have been different."

"So do I, Kathy. Good luck to you."

He gave me one last gentle look as I left his office. The compassion in that man's heart could take your breath away.

Mom rode a Greyhound bus from Denver for my graduation. She stayed at my place. By the end of her visit I'd learn the full extent of the effect my screaming had had on her several years before.

She couldn't walk long distances, so I treated her to a visit to Sea World in a wheelchair. She loves sea animals like I do. I hoped for a wonderful lasting memory between us. But while we shared the apartment I noticed that she seemed unable or unwilling to take care of herself in the most basic ways. It seemed like she didn't care about herself enough to do so. She mentioned the sense of guilt she carried for not being there for Brian and me when we were kids, and I didn't know what to say.

Then, when we said good-bye at the bus station, the look in her eyes left me with an unforgettable sense of disappointment. She didn't have a happy hug to share with me that day. Only fear and mistrust looked at me, haunting me long after. I had tried to make our visit special for her, to eradicate the effect of my verbal rampage somehow.

But after she left, I again asked the universe, "How am I ever going to make it up to her?" No one could have convinced me it would ever be possible.

Because of how I felt about my mania-driven destructive act that had shattered my spirit, along with the numbing sedation of the Zyprexa on top of depression, my graduation—what should have been my finest hour—felt like just going through the motions. I couldn't feel joy, a sense of accomplishment, or even gratitude. Nothing.

After graduation I stayed sleepy enough to not think about much of anything. I could barely do my spiritual practice once every two weeks, let alone twice a day, even with the support of a great, Panamanian, teddy bear of a friend who would come chant with me now and then. On Zyprexa my appetite for starches grew insatiable—one of its known side effects. I didn't care.

Just sleep, I thought.

And I ate.

I went in and out of the Sanford crisis unit several times the next year. Those devils were back, riding the saddle straddling my heart. On one of those visits, I made it a point to approach the head psychiatrist about what had been done to me there ten years before. I spoke to her diplomatically, with a respectful attitude. But she didn't take me seriously and just made excuses.

I hurt my back as a babysitter lifting a two-year-old. Within a year, I couldn't stand upright, but rather could only lean to my right side at a forty-five degree angle. Nor could I put weight on my right leg. I hobbled in excruciating pain to various medical doctors, physical therapy, and alternative medical practitioners until I couldn't leave my bed one morning. That day I missed a very special ceremony in which I would've witnessed a dear young friend I'd introduced to the practice become an SGI member. So instead of being at her ceremony, paramedics were carrying me down a flight of stairs to an ambulance.

I was in the hospital for several days before meeting my consulting neurosurgeon. Fear of permanently winding up in a wheelchair plagued me. But during this time I used my spiritual discipline every moment I was awake and not eating to strengthen my determination to become well. In addition, one of my leaders deeply encouraged me over the phone. Then, even though the surgeon said the chances of suc- cessful back surgery are fifty-fifty at best, I knew deep in my heart with one-hundred-percent cer- tainty during that first consult that he would help me get completely well. In fact, when we first shook hands I actually felt like I was meeting a Buddha. (Of course, everyone is a Buddha, it's just a matter of whether one is aware of it or not.)

Fortunately, a close friend took me into her home to look after me during this time. My fundamental darkness insinuated constant reservations and anxiety about going under the knife—so for two months I spent many hours a day chanting and also studied Buddhism for courage and inspiration. Finally, Ann encouraged me to trust the intuitive certainty I'd had when I met the surgeon, so I took the plunge.

After surgery, seeing me standing straight and tall with no pain, Dad's fiancé actually squealed with delight! (I got to make it to their wedding but in the hard-shell of a brace over my fancy dress. Thank goodness for that shell's protection, but what a sight!)

I returned to work again, but part time, changed to Geodon, an anti-psychotic drug that did not cause me to have severe lethargy or cravings for carbohydrates, and moved into my own apartment.

During this time, I began a friendship with the Bell family. They accepted me with all my periodic emotional volatility. Even though I was on medication, the PTSD of the "curse" played havoc with my moods and emotions, but the Bells understood, and we grew to care about each other as if we were family. The difference in our skin color made no difference to us. Practicing Buddhism together made our respect, love, compassion and appreciation for each other stem from stronger roots than the ethnic roots that often keep people from connecting on a deep level. This rich connection stemmed from our vow to attain supreme happiness and help others do the same, the very same vow that made it possible for Susan and me to rise above our difficulties years before. A rare and precious occurrence, some would say.

As a result of the Bell's encouragement, I decided to take on leadership responsibility again, supporting a small group of SGI members living near me while coordinating our chapter's study committee. This benefitted me enormously, as I'm sure the Bells knew it would. I soon felt stronger and capable enough to take on a much more challenging full-time position to overcome the fear that my brain had turned to mush. Happily, I learned it hadn't.

Then, I summoned up the confidence and determination to do a letter-writing campaign to public and political officials in my county and state and at the national level. I couldn't help but remember the woman like me who had screamed from the seclusion room within weeks of my mistreatment in there in 1993. After she got out of the room, she had boldly talked to other patients on the unit, including me, saying she was going to sue. She asked me if I would be one of her witnesses.

The coward in me emerged. "Sure," I said, knowing I wouldn't get involved. I'd been thoroughly cowed by the abuse.

Now, thirteen years later, I was writing those letters largely in memory of her and for others like us who were likely receiving similar "treatment." For all those who would, one day, need someone to take the time to listen with kindness and compassion rather than use the quicker, cheaper, traumatizing expedient of restraints to handle their freaking out on a mental ward. I received messages back from a few politicians. I was surprised when the office of the governor of Florida responded. His staff person said that a bill regarding Psychiatric Advance

Directives (PAD) to legally uphold the rights, dignity and treatment preferences of psychiatric inpatients was on his desk right then. Unfortunately, as of 2015, research indicates that Florida does not have a law on the books that designates PAD's as legal documents like some other states do.

Around this time, a nonfiction article about my life got published in what I consider to be the most significant and optimistic newspaper in the country, the *World Tribune*.[15] As a mystically synchronistic event, the date of the issue with my article, June 23, 2006, happened to be exactly ten years from the date I met my great mentor in person, on June 23, 1996, a spiritually profound turning point in my life.

As I strove to do my best at my new job, I continued fighting to believe in myself and put into practice what Nichiren teaches, to become the master of my mind rather than let my mind master me. What were those dreams of mine again? Not only had long use of psychiatric medications put up a wall as impenetrable as the Iron Curtain between me and my memories, it had also switched off my imagination and my ability to dream.

I consulted my medical psychologist and asked him to monitor me closely as I tried living without psychiatric medication for a while. Maybe my ongoing, unrelenting numbness and depression were, in part, from being on meds that weren't right for me for four long years. I provided excellent customer care at my job (I love helping people) but felt at a dead-end, feeling so dead inside. My doctor agreed to help me try living med-free, and I continued to check-in with him and my therapist regularly. Still, things weren't changing.

So I poured my heart out in a letter I faxed to President Ikeda. Then, an old movie based on the book, *Great Expectations*, inspired me to make the biggest change of my life. In the movie, the male protagonist treats the woman he had loved from afar since he was a boy as if she were *the* most special person that had ever existed.

I thought of the piece of jewelry the compassionate forces of the universe surprised me with at a laundromat back in my mid-twenties. Hanging from the metal mesh in one of the tumble dryers was a gold chain. And on that chain was a gold charm in the shape of a heart. And in that gold heart, the word "special" was written. Wow! No one had used the word special to describe me except when David told me that in high school, and I hadn't felt special for a very long time. But not just any crummy person would have been given that special gift, right?

I remembered that necklace when I watched *Great Expectations*. I thought, *I'm going to do something special for myself. I deserve it. I'm moving out of swampy, sticky-hot Florida. I'm moving to the mountains!*

Years before, while living in the rehabilitation home, I had complained to one of my young women's leaders how much I hated Florida. She asked me why I didn't move somewhere else. I thought about it but knew I didn't have the strength or courage to move away from the area, away from my SGI family. Having only practiced three years, and with what I'd just been through, I needed a lot of support back then. But now I was ready. I knew I could move away from all the people who cared about me and be ok.

I had visited friends in the rural mountains of Western North Carolina, and though I'd never been to Asheville, it made sense to move near a smallish city known to have other creative souls like me. A close friend in Orlando had once shared with me her special fondness for the town of Black Mountain, North Carolina. She'd said if she could leave Orlando and live anywhere she wished, that would be the place. I set my determination, chanted, and put an ad on Asheville's Craiglist to be a live-in nanny. I was offered just one job. In where? You guessed it. Black Mountain, North Carolina!

CHAPTER FIFTEEN

One would think moving would entail great excitement and enthusiasm. I longed for a change and wanted to feel hopeful. I even believed that I'd learn what happiness felt like in the mountains. But the heaviness of depression continued to weigh me down while I lived off the energy of anxiety to accomplish the move.

Once I finished the move, I began to hike and reach out to my mentor more often via fax. Simultaneously, I quit cigarette smoking and TV watching and quickly lost a lot of weight. My last manic attack five years earlier left me afraid to feel anything like happiness. I was certain that, if I felt happy inside, it meant mania was coming on and all hell was going to break loose.

But the mountains had a profound effect on me, as did the kind, caring nature of many of the people I met in the area. I hadn't realized all those years in Florida that a person is meant to have a *relationship* with Nature and the earth. Three separate attacks by mounds of fire ants in Florida over the years, the oppressive heat on top of my regularly scheduled hot flashes, and alligators and snakes in the lakes kept me in an air-conditioned cocoon most of the time down there. But here, I could swim outdoors. I could sit on the ground safely any time I liked. I learned that placing the top of my head onto the ground while offering gratitude had an immediate grounding effect on me. I finally had the answer to the question I had carried about my last experience in the emergency room on that gurney.

As I began my first private midnight skinny dip in a secluded lake, I had to keep telling myself, *It's okay. If you feel anything, it's not snakes or alligators, just benign aquatic life.* Through these swims and hikes along with my Buddhist practice out there, my spirit began to awaken. To soar. I was no longer numb and actually began to experience a sense of safety, since I'd not been traumatized here, and it felt nothing like crime-infested Orlando. My heart began to thaw.

For the first time I felt the rush of the creek running through my chest so that the principle of the oneness of life and the environment expounded in Buddhism became abundantly clear. Years of bottled up gratitude for my practice that I hadn't been able to feel before and praise for life, all life, including my own, began erupting in my heart like the geyser Old Faithful in Yellowstone. I listened to the earth with my all of my being, and the earth began to mentor me. I was home.

However, two months into my new job that summer a major obstacle arose. The nanny work had only provided room and board, so I'd taken on a second job at Pizza Hut. But the mother I worked for didn't like that I might not be available every time she needed me. I assured her that my manager promised to work around my nanny schedule. But in early August she gave me written notice that I was terminated. Shocked and scared, I only had less than a month to find affordable living arrangements and enough work to support myself. Anxiety overwhelmed me. But I returned to my practice fiercely determined to overcome these new difficulties rather than be controlled by fear and doubt.

Within a week I had a great apartment and a new job. In Florida, I'd moved about every other year for the previous ten years, so finding an apartment and location so right for me that I've stayed here for over eight years says a lot. And I loved my new job as a Direct Care Educator with developmentally disabled kids. I'd long wanted to try that kind of work. Two of my uncles were that way, one with Down's Syndrome.

Working with these children brought my head into alignment with my heart. With one child who could only respond yes or no with his hands, I experienced the Buddhist concept of the interconnectedness of all life. I learned to listen to my intuition to understand him and see that I was as open-hearted towards him as he was with me. I began to comprehend why someone had recently told me my life was like a radio-tower transmitter. Serving this twelve-year-old, I became able, like him, to live in the present moment. Helping him overcome his behavioral challenges with positive reinforcement helped me recognize and overcome my own behavior challenges with equally gentle compassion. I actually began caring enough to brush and floss my teeth every day, something I'd never been capable of in my life.

Unfortunately, without the stabilizing influence of medication, I went overboard in a frenzy of manic energy and carelessly reinjured my back lifting his seventy-five pounds. My surgeon had warned me to be careful after my back surgery, but the stress of two jobs generated a speedy manic energy that didn't allow me to be careful enough.

Simultaneously delivery driving for Pizza Hut also became overwhelming. Not only were cuts spontaneously appearing all over my hands due to the stress (a physical malady I inherited from my father), I also began getting confused trying to find the houses.

Manic energy, depression, anxiety, paranoia, and my budding sense of intuitive awareness took turns dominating my decisions and actions. I didn't try to apply for workers' compensation. I was eventually able to work with other children again, but at the time, I wasn't sure what was worse: wrenching my back or feeling wrenched away from the young boy who had taught me such wonderful lessons in the meaningful silences between us.

That first year I also started volunteering at a community radio station in Asheville. Finally, I had a way to put my communications degree to work—as a radio news broadcast journalist. And not for just any program. For *The Global Report—Radio Edition*, where we focused on researching, editing, and reporting on all the under-reported news the mass media overlooks or ignores.

For years, my father had repeatedly suggested I read the newspaper on a regular basis, even daily like he did. I would read it once in a while, but usually just headlines or the first few paragraphs of a news story. Now, I was reading complete news stories all throughout the week, every week. Our team searched through all sorts of credible news sources. Reading many articles took me hours to research, edit to under two-minute segments, and record.

I loved the challenge of the work, but it was hard learning so many sad things about the world, about so many injustices. That could make anyone go off the deep end, especially someone struggling with a disorder like mine. It certainly made me shaky. But as disheartening as the news was, it was also the shock that I needed. Depression and television had kept my head in the sand for "eons" except in the safety zone of my spiritual community. Since taking part in a sit-in at boarding school in tenth grade, I hadn't been involved in activism except for the various activities our sangha initiated for environmental, social justice, and peace initiatives. Now, I lived in an area where lots of people volunteer and take altruistic action in their community to make a difference. It was time for me to get busy too.

A number of folks at the station were heavily involved in activism, so they really got me fired up. Now was my chance to take the action I hadn't had the consciousness to do in college. A number of station volunteers walked spiritual paths that intrigued me too, so I learned from their wisdom and compassion. And like some of them, I began participating in various community initiatives.

After working at the station a while, though, it became obvious I needed to focus on doing mostly positive news stories. And not just for my own sanity. People needed to hear them, to know so many positive actions are being taken behind the scenes by citizens every day, in every country, including right here in the U.S. The public especially needed to hear these stories in the U.S., where bad news and sensationalism that attempts to sway people's perspectives dominate *not all* but a lot of the mass media so much of the time. For two and a half years, I put my sometimes cheerful, sometimes passionate voice on the airwaves for the greater good and built-up my self-esteem in the process.

CHAPTER SIXTEEN

During the fall of my first year in North Carolina, I received a call from my favorite aunt.

"Kathy, your mom is in the hospital."

"What? I just talked to her on her birthday last month, and she was fine. What happened?"

"Well, she's catatonic, unable to speak or eat or respond in any way. And the worst of it is the doctors don't know what's causing it."

"Oh my God, Aunt Jean!"

The first thing I thought to do was ask friends for support with their prayers and healing energy for Mom. Then, a young man I'd worked with at Pizza Hut, who wanted more than anything to get out of the mountains for a while and see the country, drove with me out to Denver to see her. We took off on our adventure, but due to hyper-mania I decided to take a detour first.

While my young friend stayed with Terry in Omaha, I drove hundreds of miles out of our way to see the live radio performance of *A Prairie Home Companion* in St. Paul, Minnesota. I had to meet the host of the show, Garrison Keillor, with whom I'd been communicating telepathically for some months. But, upon meeting him after the show, he didn't treat me any differently than any of his other fans—didn't even seem to recognize me.

This is outrageous! I thought. I stormed out of the theatre after one of his body guards made sure I didn't try to approach Garrison a second time. How humiliating. *Am I really that far gone into mania?* I wondered.

My young friend and I made it to Denver and entered Mom's rehab facility. She had come out of the catatonia in the hospital during the few days of our trip. I recognized her profile as she sat in her wheelchair in the hallway.

"Hi, Mom!" I said.

She turned to look at me and smiled real big with surprise when she realized it was me. No one had known we were coming.

"How are you?" I asked.

But she couldn't talk. She couldn't utter a word. She started to make the sound of the beginning of the word "good" but couldn't really get the "guh" out. My heart ached.

I took out a gift I'd brought for her. She and I have always shared a love of dolphins.

"Here, Mom, can I put this on you?" I showed her the dolphin-shaped turquoise and silver earring in my hand.

She nodded.

As I put it in her earlobe I said, "I'm going to keep the other earring, so we'll both always have one that keeps us connected to each other."

I wheeled her into her room and asked if my friend and I could do the practice while she listened. She nodded.

Afterward, I asked, "Mom, is it okay if I massage you a little?"

She nodded and smiled.

I bent over her and massaged her shoulders and arms and then moved to the front of her wheelchair, crouched down, and massaged her legs.

As I did so, I reminded her of some good memories I had of us together. "Remember when we went detassling in the corn fields when I visited you those two summers? What was that song we sang? Oh yeah, 'We are the go-fer girls.' Even as hot as it was, that was some fun we had together, wasn't it?"

She nodded and breathed out a contented sigh.

"I never told you this, but I thought those Halloween costumes you made for Brian and me when I was in third grade were incredible. I was so proud to know I had a mother who could make us look like computers out of big cardboard boxes. We hardly fit in your two-door 'Orange Bomb' Pinto but, since it was the early 1970s, you were definitely a woman ahead of your time with those costumes." Somehow, even as young as I was, I had known that.

She chuckled and nodded. Another big

smile.

I paused for a while, thinking. I remembered the anger in Mom's voice all those years whenever the subject of my father came up between us. I reflected on how awful she said things had been between her and Dad when she was pregnant with me. Like when she accidentally dropped some raw eggs on the kitchen floor. Trying to clean them up, she started gagging and asked Dad for help. She said they were making her sick, that she was about to vomit. But he just said, since she dropped them, she'd have to clean them up herself, and then he went down to his workshop in the cellar.

So now, as I knelt down in front of her, holding her hands, I said with great tenderness, "Mom, you've really got to forgive Dad. Holding onto that anger towards him all these years has really hurt you. I know he treated you badly, but it's been forty years and you've just got to let it go."

She looked down at me for a minute, smiled, and nodded her head. She was going to do it. She was going to forgive him! And, as soon as she let me know that, I felt a release in my own heart. Angst flew out of my heart, and a light, healing energy emerged. I knew I had accomplished my mission with her that day and had begun making up for the pain.

CHAPTER SEVENTEEN

A few weeks after I got home, my aunt called me again. "Kathy, your mom's back in the hospital. She's having the same symptoms as last time. She's catatonic, and the doctors don't know what's causing it this time either."

Right away, I asked my SGI community for their support. But this time, I didn't stop there. I faxed my mentor a letter asking for his support for Mom, too, from him and his friends. I wrote that there was no telling whether she would live or not and shared about the severe anger and depression that had isolated her for such a long time. I wrote that I hoped she would live many more years, so I could help make the remaining years of her life happy ones.

I soaked a lot of Kleenexes that night and journaled out my feelings and thoughts. That made it possible for me to concentrate fully on my practice. As I chanted, a vision came to my mind that I was a being of light. I was entering Mom's mind where she stood alone and afraid in the middle of a dark forest. I saw myself as that light-being leading her out of the forest into the light.

(Someone later remarked that this seemed similar to a technique of shamanism.)

The next day, my aunt called to say Mom was awake, eating and talking, and the doctors couldn't explain what happened.

A few weeks later, my aunt and I spoke again, and she said, "It's really remarkable. Your mother is like a totally different person now ever since she woke up."

"What do you mean?" I asked.

"She's so positive. As you know, before this she had been angry and depressed for many years. She didn't like to spend time with people at all. She mostly kept to herself and isolated. But now, she's so happy. It's really hard to believe the change in her."

"Wow, Aunt Jean. That is so wonderful to hear! Many of my friends and I have been chanting for her. I'm so grateful she's doing so well."

She didn't take too kindly to hearing that we'd chanted for Mom. In fact, she poo-poo'd the idea that it might've helped. But a month or so later she actually said, "You should definitely keep up the chanting. Seeing how much your mom has changed, it obviously works."

How tickled I was to hear her say that.

During and after Mom's healing, I felt so profoundly grateful to everyone for their help. What a rare thing. Helping Mom have a change in the depths of her life in this way changed something deep in me, as if in saving her from a life of terrible suffering, we both were saved together. With deep appreciation for Mom, I've come to treasure that which we share genetically, those ways in which I take after her. Especially my creativity.

By communing with Nature and simultaneously fusing with the melodious Nam-myoho-renge-kyo, I unlocked the harmonies and poetry in my heart. Songs started emerging from my life *a lot*. Much more than ever before. Music reflecting the issues in the news that haunted me the most, like "Remember Dorian Grey (Indictment of War Profiteers)." "Fairy Forest" in which I sing out for justice in a very personal way. And then, also, fun songs that reflect my gratitude to nature and encourage my growing community of friends. I could finish the song I'd started in Florida—"What Is True Happiness?" And then my sense of humor began to bloom.

A sense of humor. Really? Me? Yep! It became emboldened every time I went up to my Mountain Mama sanctuary. I might hike up there huffing and puffing to get out my anxious energy, but I descended from those heights the greatest comedian ever.

Yes, I could actually *enjoy* my own company. Let go of the seriousness of life and be fun for a change. What a wonderful love affair with Earth I developed. The child in me nurtured in Nature's embrace. My sacred imagination restored and whole, being shared with others like those who liked to sing along to my songs.

And Mom's psychic change wasn't just temporary. She became so friendly, well-liked and appreciated in her care facility that soon the staff asked her to be the President of the Resident Council for over one hundred residents. It was a position she took very seriously for over a year. She sought to know what the residents thought and needed in order to represent them well. I was

so delighted that she could start to feel proud of
herself, to live with such a sense of dignity and
self-respect.

CHAPTER EIGHTEEN

I had no idea that moving to the mountains would shake up my life so much. The loss of my nanny job and the experience with Mom were actually just the beginning. But building indestructible happiness in the depths of my life would, necessarily, take overcoming one obstacle after another. To become unshakably strong and undefeatable.

By this time, I had stayed off psychiatric medication for almost two years. I was far from safe. Every second to third week, I'd be inconsolably depressed, unable to call anyone or leave my bed and apartment for days at a time. This continually re-infected me with a sense of worthlessness, powerlessness, and hopelessness.

A plague of hyper-mania came upon me. I still kept thinking I was communicating telepathically back and forth with Mr. Keillor. Signs in my environment and simple body movements I enacted, like scratching an itch, continually distracted me with paranoid thoughts about what they meant. And during grandiose phases it seemed that every time the weather changed, it was because my mood changed. Since the sensible part of me was never convinced any of this was true, the conflict between this common sense and these hyper-manic thoughts made me very afraid. *Am I crazy?* I thought anxiously.

And then in hypomania, moods of euphoria and irritability took turns dominating me. The obsessive worry about everything, with negative thoughts about many people I knew, including myself, certainly didn't reflect my Buddhist values. I felt open and vulnerable to environmental stimuli and other's feelings constantly. I went on spending sprees with credit cards like money was free.

I quickly learned to stay away from radio programs with commercials. Due to car commercials, I wound up sitting across from a Toyota salesman trying to convince him that if he gave me a car, like a free leasing arrangement, my great (grandiose) reputation would convince many other people to buy the very same expensive model he gave me for free. Oddly enough, he didn't go for my proposal.

I drove to Florida for a conference and to see Dad. He was in the hospital. While in Orlando, I looked at police photo albums for a picture of Rocky the rapist. Because the mountains helped me feel my innate dignity and the sanctity of my life, my Buddha nature, I became aware of the importance of taking action about this perpetrator's crime. Other than telling people about them, there was little I could do about the four-point restraint crimes against me because the statute of limitations had run out long ago. The statute had also run out on the sexual assault. But if I identified Rocky's mug shot because he had been arrested for hurting another woman or was wanted for such a crime, I might be able to help. I hadn't realized my responsibility twenty years ago to stop Rocky. But I could take responsibility now. Even if my efforts came to no avail, I had to do the right thing.

The Orlando police department researched their database and forwarded numerous photos of known rapists from the 1980's and 90's to the Black Mountain police. Rocky's picture wasn't among them, which could mean several things. I hope it indicates the most optimistic possibility, that he never raped another woman again.

For me, the search in itself was powerfully transformative. Not only was I beginning to take action outside the SGI for justice at community, national and international levels. (Active at all three levels, The Global Report-Radio Edition was played on stations in other states and on the internet.) Now, I was also acting for justice in a very personal way. This simple act eliminated the guilt I'd long carried for not reporting the rape. It also diminished the shame I felt from mistakenly thinking I was in any way to blame for what happened; my sense of self-worth grew.

After I returned from Florida, I took another trip, this time to New York City to see the Broadway musical *The Color Purple* on a chartered bus with an African-American Baptist congregation.

What a blast going off on my own to the New York Metropolitan Museum of Art! It opened my eyes to the aliveness one can see in the eyes of portraits by the great masters. I didn't know their original paintings could do that. I'd never read in books that one could have such an experience with great art or seen that effect in paintings that I'd viewed in galleries.

On the bus trip itself, I drew from my many chartered bus excursions with the SGI and orchestrated open-mike sessions. My fellow travelers and I enjoyed performances, sing-alongs, and ensuing discussions rather than all of us just staring mutely at the video-feed of DVD movies for the entire trip. I developed friendships with some of the people I'd gotten to know. And although the trip was pretty inexpensive, these personal exchanges made our lives richer in a way that money can't buy.

Not long after that, I traveled to South Carolina to see the Democratic nominee for the 2008 presidential election. While driving back from Mr. Obama's speech, I hit a deer on a rainy night at two in the morning. The deer and I both walked away, but my car limped quite badly.

That night I also saw the truth of the mass fast-food market. Live chickens transported in tiny cages on a huge semi-truck under the cover of darkness. Jammed in there like sardines on top of each other. Hundreds of little, sad, black eyes staring out at me made me get much more committed to making food choices based on my conscience. I needed to consider the origin of what I would be consuming, including the difference between organic and genetically modified foods. I never imagined the misery we put animals through to get a fast-food meal. Now, I would never forget.

Then, on March 14th, 2008, I couldn't find a parking place near the radio station. I parked in a reserved lot next to the station, just long enough to run up and ask my producer where else I might park.

"Hi, Ed. The parking garage next door is full, and all the metered spaces on the street are taken. Do you know any other places I can park?"

He gave me some suggestions that were a few blocks away. I said thanks and was about to run back to my car when a volunteer I didn't know greeted me.

"I just finished this nonviolence training course in Tennessee...here." She handed me a pamphlet. "I can't say enough good things about it." She pointed to the brochure. "This tells you everything you'll want to know. It only costs thirty-five dollars for the two-day course."

"Oh, really? That seems right up my alley." I'd researched about Gandhi's life in college. Getting trained in nonviolence techniques seemed a great idea. "But I'd really better get back to my car and find a place to park."

I left and approached my car. Then I began to run.

"No! Please, don't tow away my car! I wasn't even there ten minutes!"

A rotund man with a cigarette dangling from his lips said, "No way. I've already started hooking you up. I can't stop now."

I raced around my car to look at the towing apparatus. He hadn't completed his hookup yet. I still had a chance! I placed my foot in between the apparatus and my left front car tire.

"If you don't move away from the car, I'm going to call the police!"

I called a friend on my cell phone to ask for her help.

"That seems like a good idea," she said, "putting your foot there to delay the tow truck. I read in the paper that just last week the Asheville city council had been approached by outraged residents decrying these predatory towing tactics."

This was like stoking the embers of my inner flame of justice. I couldn't turn back now. A mental picture of my mentor came to mind, the one taken just after he was released from a Japanese jail after being arrested and detained for two weeks on trumped up charges of election fraud. As the youth at the forefront of the Soka Gakkai's efforts to empower people, his efforts raised the hackles of the Japanese establishment. The authorities actually threatened to arrest his frail mentor if he didn't admit to the false charges. Nothing was more important to him than protecting his mentor, so he complied with their demands. It took him four long years in court to prove his innocence.

Thinking of Dr. Ikeda's courage motivated me to stand up on behalf of all those outraged citizens. I wasn't the only one whose paycheck didn't cover all her monthly bills, who had to go to the food bank just to get by. I wasn't the only one who didn't have the $150 the tow-truck driver said I'd have to pay to get my car out of the impound lot. But then again, I *was* the only one who needed her car to pick up her developmentally disabled client from school later that day.

Let the police come, I thought. *Surely, they will listen to reason.*

The first officer was nice enough, but I didn't budge, and he apparently couldn't or wouldn't sway the tow-truck driver on my behalf. Then, a second officer arrived—a morbidly obese, short woman with yellow hair. She didn't want any guff.

She said, "If you give the man $125 now, you will save $25, and you can keep your car instead of him towing it off."

It didn't seem fair, but I considered doing just that.

I saw an African-American woman dressed in a nurse's uniform talking with the male officer. She smiled sympathetically at me from the other side of my car, trying to reason with him on my behalf.

"Okay," I said, thinking fast. "Why don't I give my debit card to this nurse, and she can run up the street and get out the $100 I have in the bank." To be exact, $110 was all I had. But ATM's don't dispense anything less than twenty dollar bills. I figured I could get the other $25 somehow. With the nurse's help, at least I'd have the bulk of the money.

"No," the yellow-haired officer said. "You have to go and get the money yourself."

With high anxiety, I thought for a moment. "But officer, if I leave my car to go get the money, how do I know you won't have my car towed by the time I get back?"

The female officer muttered some epithet and *BAM*! It was as if a football linebacker slammed into my side.

"Get the Taser, get the Taser!" she barked to the other officer when he joined her to force me onto the ground. But with all the strength I could muster I resisted and they didn't get me all the way face down on the pavement. I didn't want my face down there!

Caught up in the drama, I yelled, "You can't crush my spirit! I won't let you!"

"We're not trying to crush you," she said.

Somehow that didn't ring true.

Handcuffed in the back seat of the policewoman's patrol car, I felt something in the palm of my right hand. They'd taken all my belongings, including my purse with my cell phone in it. What they didn't know was that, in my bipolar condition, months earlier, I'd purchased two cell phones from two different companies. It was extremely important I have one for business and one for personal use, vital for my success. I was sure of that at the time even though I couldn't afford such excesses. But it turned out that this foolish purchase actually helped me. I still had my black "business" cell phone cradled in the palm of my hand! The police had never noticed it.

In the patrol car with plastic handcuffs tying my wrists tightly together behind my back, I stretched my arms to the right and leaned over to get my mouth close to the phone. I called my supervisor and left a voicemail that something had happened to my car, and I wouldn't be able to pick up my client that afternoon.

I started to make a second call, but the officers were on me, trying to wrestle the phone out of my grasp. With the bottoms of my feet wedged against the back of the front seat, they couldn't get at my hands behind my back. Even after her second threat of, "Where's the Taser? Where's the Taser?!" to the other officer, I wasn't relinquishing my phone. It was all that connected me to the possibility of help.

The female bully officer got into the driver's seat and said, "It doesn't matter. We'll get it from you at the jail."

I knew she was right. But at least I could make one more call to let someone know what was happening to me.

Then I noticed the nurse's car ahead of the tow truck wasn't moving. The female officer left the patrol car to speak to her.

Flinging her arms and pointing, she demanded, "Get your car out of here, or I'll have you arrested too!"

I later learned the nurse's intention: to stop the tow truck from taking my car away.

Released on my own recognizance after going before the judge, I stopped to speak to the female bully officer who was standing at the jail's exit doors. Instead of being angry like I was earlier, I remembered the Japanese educator, first Soka Gakkai President Tsunesaburo Makiguchi, who was tortured by the Japanese government authorities in a Japanese prison during World War II. Rather than capitulate to the military government's coercion to support Japan's war efforts by worshipping Shinto, the government's religion, he had refused and protected the purity of Nichiren Buddhism. Even though the persecution was so severe that he died in that prison, he still compassionately discussed with his guards and the prosecutors who interrogated him about the correctness of this philosophy. Demonstrating his great inner freedom and happiness, he dialogued with them to convince them that they could become happy too. My situation was light-years from that horrific injustice, but the thought of Mr. Makiguchi's actions prompted me to share Nam-myoho-renge-kyo with the officer.

Now I knew this wasn't an opportunity to elaborate about the practice. I only shared for a moment that chanting helps people become truly happy. But her response was shocking. With her eyes wide and a bright smile on her face, she thanked me for telling her. Was I seeing her Buddha nature? Her surprise was obvious. I wasn't mumbling epithets about her under my breath or giving her mean looks. I'm sure others had, and she probably earned those complaints. Had she been waiting at the exit door to revel in the anger she'd stirred up in me? No matter. She may be dominated by the life-states of animality and anger, but that didn't mean I had to be. My mentor didn't raise me that way.

CHAPTER NINETEEN

At my court appearance, I was forced to sit on the floor against the side wall just ten feet or so from the District Attorney since all two hundred seats were taken that morning. Naively, I took out my laptop, glad I'd brought something to do to pass the time. With all those people, it looked like I was going to be there a while.

As I opened my laptop, I noticed the bailiff pointing at me. I didn't comprehend his sign language.

Then, all of a sudden, he stomped over, towered over me, and shouted, "Do you want to go to jail?!"

Well, that alone would be intimidating to anyone, but it had only been a month since I'd been assaulted by someone in a uniform much like he was wearing. On top of that, I'd gotten barely two hours sleep the night before due to the anxiety I felt about the next day's court appearance.

You can imagine my state of mind as I was

being yelled at. Shock and horror froze me to the spot. Panicked, my heart also blazed with outrage. Why was he yelling at me? What had I done?

The bailiff stepped back a few feet to see my reaction. Not wishing to make noise and disturb the court, I raised my arms, palms up, to ask him what was wrong.

He stared at me furiously, lowered his voice, and said, "Put your laptop away."

Instead of complying, my head swirled in confusion, and I whispered, "Why?"

I could not fathom the correct measures to take. All I needed to do was put my laptop away, and he'd have left me alone. Instead, I sat there staring at him with a confounded look on my face. By the time I finally got it and followed his instructions, it was too late.

He held me in handcuffs in the front of the courtroom for what seemed like a long time. With two hundred people looking on I felt humiliated. But I knew I had not intentionally caused the disruption. Even so, I made an apology to the judge. I didn't think I'd done anything to warrant being arrested, but my nerves warned me to say the most respectful thing. I had been woefully ignorant as to courtroom decorum—that no electronic devices or even reading materials were allowed in court. Ignorance cost me dearly this time.

Walking with the bailiff to the jail, I said, "I didn't know laptops weren't allowed in court. Sorry about the mix-up. I got hardly any sleep last night, and my anxiety from being assaulted recently, on top of a disorder I have, made me confused and frightened when all this happened. I hope you understand."

"Well, uh, now that you've explained, I can see why you acted the way you did." He responded to my respectful attitude with openness.

Sitting in front of the judge's window in the jail, I explained what happened. On the way to the jail, I had asked the bailiff if he would please say a word on my behalf when I went before the judge. He kindly agreed to do so and, after the judge was finished with me, I looked to the bailiff, and he did just that.

Immediately following my appearance before the judge, I was again released on my own recognizance, but now with a third misdemeanor charge to deal with.

I shared my story with a local ACLU lawyer at a gathering where he was speaking to the homeless about their rights regarding police actions against them. He sympathized with my situation and offered some advice, but he didn't believe my case warranted their involvement.

Then, one day, I was sitting on the bus. I decided to use the bus to travel to Asheville since driving my car was killing me in the cost of gas. I could also make a cause that way, however small, for the environment. And I liked meeting people on the bus.

As I rode, awaiting my stop, the woman across from me said, "Hey, aren't you that lady who was arrested by the police that day with the tow truck?"

"Yes, that was me. How did you know?" I peered at her closely.

"Oh, you don't recognize me. I'm not in my

uniform. But it was me that day that tried to talk to the officers and help you out."

"Oh, my gosh. Really? It was you?"

"Yes. That was me."

"I can't believe you noticed me just now."

"Oh, that was something I'll never forget."

"Well, I can't thank you enough for trying to help me like that. Not many people would have. It's amazing you got involved. My name's Kat. What's yours?" (Having never felt good being called "Kathy," I first called myself "Kat" after my move and then settled on "Kitty" sometime after this incident. Friends had suggested Kitty fit my personality. And after trying it on for a while it felt like a good fit to me too.)

The woman told me her name and said, "Well, I don't believe in turning a blind eye when someone's in trouble, and you sure weren't getting a fair shake as far as I could see. You told them you needed your car for work, that you didn't have the money. And you were only parked there for a few minutes. I didn't understand why they couldn't have let you slide."

"Did you think I was being nasty or belligerent to the police?"

"Oh, no. If anything, you were being nice and respectful. There was no call for that policewoman to assault you like that. That was just horrible!"

"Would you be willing to write up a statement for me or something?"

"Well now, I would. But you know, I don't want no trouble or nothin'. They get my name, and it could cause all kinds of trouble."

"Oh, well, that's ok. I understand." And I actually understood her concerns very well. Ever since I began telling people what the police had done to me, like at local CopWatch and other community meetings, I began hearing horrendous stories of abuses the police had done to others in the area. Though I'd wished she would've wanted to support me further, I couldn't blame her for wanting to stay anonymous.

We both exited the bus at the terminal, so

I thanked her again and said good-bye.

I met with my public defender, but he had no sympathy for my situation. He seemed to think I should just take my lumps and not fight any of this. Certainly that would have been the easiest thing for him. But I was hoping for more.

About this time, I brought a homeless guy with schizophrenia to stay in my apartment for a time. This was the opposite of a good idea. I'd been friends with schizophrenics before, so I knew it was normal for him to mumble to himself a lot. But being in such close quarters it freaked me out. Within a day or so, I began yelling at him and thought medicating myself was the answer. But a wise friend suggested that rather than taking psychiatric medication to deal with how I was feeling around this guy, maybe I should look at changing the situation. Even though I thought it was a good idea to ask him to leave, I didn't want to kick him out.

I'd stayed faithful to my mental health medical appointments after moving. My psy-chiatric nurse practitioner was getting worried though. Hikes, communing with nature, my spiritual discipline, individual therapy, and more weren't enough to keep my spirit grounded, to keep my extreme anxiety and psychotic thoughts at bay. Now, this rage with this homeless guy in my apartment.

"Would you consider trying Lithium Carbonate again?" she asked.

I agonized over the decision.

Outside one night as I sat on the grass, offering tears of gratitude and praise, once again, for now living in such a profoundly supportive environment, for the loving natural energy that surrounded me, I simultaneously cried out in desperation. "What should I do?" I asked. "I'm doing everything I know how to get myself well, but I keep failing and falling backwards. I need to feel in control of myself! Isn't there something that can help me?"

Suddenly, I noticed the answer in the sky above me. Very clearly spelled out up there in the clouds were two letters. A capital "R" and a lower case "x." Yes "Rx." With the "x" attached to the "R" as in the universal symbol in the English language for prescription medication. You can imagine my amazement, awe, and wonder.

It was as if the benevolent functions and forces in the infinitely compassionate universe were reassuring me, saying, "No, you won't be a failure. Even living in this holistic, spiritual, and natural healing mecca, some people need psychiatric medication. It's okay if you try meds again. We know it's scary, but somehow you'll be okay."

So then, I thought, *Okay, I will. And maybe it will only need to be for a little while anyway.*

My nurse practitioner had already given me a prescription for the Lithium. I got it filled. I took it for three days. I'd promised myself that if it did what I remembered it did in Florida so many years before, I'd give myself permission to stop it.

Unfortunately, it did. My imagination disappeared. My juicy creativity dried up. And my wonderful sense of gratitude for life shriveled. It was as if my heart had been a butterfly yanked back into a smothering, dark cocoon. Sealed up tight in there, I felt utterly numb. I saw no animal shapes in clouds anymore, could see no images in my mind's eye, my imagination was obliterated. A chemically-induced prison of the mind is a living hell in the heart.

It seemed like forever, those few days waiting for those thousands of milligrams of Lithium to leave my system. Grateful to feel alive again, I wondered all over again, *What am I going to do now?* Fortunately for him, the homeless guy had already split.

I longed to have this nightmarish existence removed from my mind. I began to feel haunted by the radio. I almost bolted to the emergency room several times. But fear of unknown psych wards kept me away.

I attended a speech given by Michelle Obama at a local college, and taking along an 8-year-old developmentally disabled African American girl I worked with felt like a good idea. After the speech, I met a petite young woman with haunted eyes from South Carolina. We happened on a conversation about four-point restraints, and she confided she had left South Carolina and her family to find a sense of safety in Asheville after experiencing torture in restraints on a psych ward there. And then sometime later, a young friend of mine who asked me to teach her about Buddhism, a little wisp of a thing herself, shared her experience of being tied down in restraints in the ER, right here in an Asheville hospital.

No, I wasn't going to be at the mercy of that again if I could help it. And I felt sure I'd start smoking cigarettes again, too, if I were hospitalized, just like every other time. It invariably took me years to quit each time I started. No, even if I wasn't able to sleep well enough, even if all the warning bells were going off in my head, going into a psych ward again was out of the question.

Meanwhile, I became determined to change my public defender's mind, and chanted Nam-myoho-renge-kyo to be able to convince him to fight for me. Then, what do you know? Although I didn't ride the bus into Asheville often since I usually needed my car, I actually bumped into the nurse on the bus *again*. But this time I had my handy digital voice recorder with me. I interviewed her and recorded everything. I brought it to my public defender so he could see I wasn't lying. I hadn't made my story up. The pictures of the bruises on my arm taken with the newspaper the day after the assault had a story behind them now. This, along with mentioning the well-respected ACLU lawyer I had consulted, who had become something of an admirer of mine by then, got my public defender to go to bat in earnest for me.

While all this happened, I told my therapist I was going to make a formal complaint to the police department about the bully officer's actions.

Thankfully, my therapist protected me and advised, "Drain the swamp first."

It was such a strange reference I did a double take. "Huh?"

She elaborated, "Get your situation with those charges against you resolved before you take up a fight with those alligators," referring to the police and their lawyers.

Having lived in Florida, the alligator reference hit home. It could cause me a lot of grief to go after one of their own before my charges were dealt with.

So I waited.

I had my complaint form, copies of the witness's recording, copies of the pictures of my bruises. I was ready.

The results of my court case involving the three charges of the two incidents weren't completely to my liking, but it ended the best it could considering the circumstances and how little I knew. The Assistant District Attorney handling my case was the same ADA that had witnessed my courtroom arrest. So she was sure I was guilty of that charge.

I'd submitted a letter to the court about having been assaulted by someone and that I'd been dealing with the anxicty of that assault the day I was arrested in court. But the ADA would not let that charge drop. So I was offered a plea deal that the first two charges regarding the towing incident would be dropped if I accepted a Prayer for Judgment Continuance for the third charge.

My Public Defender said a PJC for the third charge was a lot better than going to court. And he assured me it would not show up as a conviction on my record, emphasizing that the ADA could make sure I looked guilty for that third charge. Somewhere along the way I'd learned that the other two charges could get expunged from my record later on. But my PD's assurance that a PJC was not the same as a conviction had me convinced that taking the deal was the best idea.

However, I discovered later that this was not true. In North Carolina, a PJC is generally considered a conviction. The PD had either been unaware or had lied to get my case over with. Being misinformed, I thought I could get the PJC overturned later on, which was a lot better than three permanent misdemeanor convictions. Certainly better for any future employment. So I took the plea.

I later learned that this happens a lot to people with minor infractions. With the court wielding so much power, we take a plea deal because those representing the system tell us it's the best we can get. In reality many people could possibly win these kinds of misdemeanor cases if they insist on a trial. Considering that the ADA in my court case was also the ADA that witnessed the laptop incident, for all I know that might have been considered a conflict of interest that could have resulted in my case being thrown out. But I didn't know nothin'.

But now that my court case was over, it was time for me to head to the Asheville P.D. Internal Affairs department with my evidence. I met with the IA officer and left him copies of my evidence. But after several weeks no one had gotten back to me. Rather than let it go for the police to deal with, as I'm sure some people would, I wouldn't. So I made my second trip to the police station. In what felt like a little interrogation room, I sat face to face across from the female officer's sergeant.

Strangely enough, he appeared to be nervous.

At first I thought, *This can't be. He says he's a twenty-year veteran of the police force, but he's squirming in his chair a lot and sweating. Is he anxious about this?* But then I reasoned to myself, *He's viewed my evidence. He knows I could make a big stink. He probably figures he's got to convince me not to press charges. So much is riding on what he does with me right now. He knows I'm not a pushover, and I could sue the department. No wonder he's worried.*

In my heart, I felt rather sorry for the man. He wasn't the one that physically assaulted me without just cause and threatened me with a Taser. No, but he was her supervisor, and he had to clean up the mess his subordinate had made.

I spoke softly and courteously. "So, have you seen the evidence and the report I filed about your subordinate's gross mishandling of the situation with the tow truck, Sergeant?" I asked after we'd made our introductions.

"Yes, Ma'am."

"Well, what I wish to know is, what has been done about this. Has the officer been reprimanded? She should at least be required to have counseling and compassion training."

"Unfortunately, Ma'am, North Carolina law prohibits the public from being informed of whether or not any officer is reprimanded and how that reprimand is carried out. It's just the law, Ma'am."

"Just what can you tell me then?" I asked.

"Really, not much. I have heard the tape of the alleged witness that you provided our Internal Affairs officer. And I've seen the picture of the bruises that you allege the assault left on you. Though I can't tell you what action has been taken about this, I can tell you something has been done. It has been addressed."

"Well, that's something at least. After all, as you heard on the recorded testimony, the witness said that I did nothing to provoke such violent aggression. In fact, you may recall, she emphasized that I was just trying to figure out a way to get all the money the tow truck driver demanded to keep my car from being towed."

"Yes, Ma'am. What was your witness's name, by the way? We'd like it for our records."

"I can't tell you that, Sergeant. She asked me not to. You understand." No way was I giving him that information. I may only have been a community radio station *volunteer* journalist, but I took protecting one's sources seriously, same as any good professional journalist would.

"Okay, Ma'am."

It seemed sneaky of him to try to get the name of my witness, but I didn't dwell on it. I continued, "Sure, at first I was standing up for justice against the predatory towing tactics that Asheville citizens have been outraged about. But then your officers convinced me I needed to pay the towing company, or I couldn't keep my car. Without my car, my client would be stranded. That motivated me more. I was trying to resolve the situation. So then, what sense does it make for them to tackle me to the ground, threaten to Taser me, and then arrest me and haul me off to jail? How was any of that warranted? Can you tell me that?"

"I'm sorry, Ma'am. I really can't speak to that. I'm sorry for your situation though."

"Well, I'd really like to ask your subordinate some questions. To have a talk with her. But I'm betting your department wouldn't support such an interaction, would it?"

"No, Ma'am, I'm afraid that's correct. We

couldn't arrange such a thing. No, Ma'am."

I wanted to ask him if he had any idea just how frustrating it is to be slapped with charges and too poor to hire my own attorney. Then once a public defender was appointed, to have to fight like hell to convince him of my innocence. Not to mention having to deal with the mental and emotional trauma from the assault.

"You cannot imagine how difficult an experience this has been for me."

"Yes, Ma'am. I'm sorry about that."

"So, there's no way at all for me to talk with this officer?"

"No, Ma'am."

And with that, I thanked the sergeant and left the building.

What he didn't know was that I'd seen the officer since the day she'd tackled me. I'd seen her at the same mental health agency where I received services. I couldn't deny the evidence. She was getting counseling. And that's at least one of the things I'd hoped would come out of all this.

The irony didn't escape me either. That I felt quite confident and in control, completely devoid of fear while sitting across from this sergeant who had been so nervous.

Going into the little room with him, I hadn't anticipated much of anything resulting from our discussion. And I didn't believe that a lawsuit was the answer. I just had to try to make a difference. To point out a grievous error and hope he'd help ensure it wouldn't happen to others by his subordinate.

But the sergeant acted so uneasy and apologetic, it affected me deeply. I actually wound up getting something big out of what I did that day.

As I walked out the doors of that police station, I remembered my many tastes of terror— the voices, needles, and shrinking feelings. The police who'd hauled me out of the walk-in crisis center in handcuffs at eighteen. The wardens of my first psych ward that tied me down. The rapist. The second four-point restraint torture.

Other horribly self-destructive acts I had perpetrated against myself and experiencing severe PTSD from "the curse" of breaking ten thousand mirrors.

Lastly, I remembered that conversation I'd had with Aunt Jean after she read the article I'd published in 2006. She described my very first taste of terror, the one I would never remember but which had happened all the same. The story that was the secret of my birth. The secret I hadn't known for more than forty years. The secret that sentenced me to live what felt like the unluckiest of lives.

This is what she told me:

I was born into the clutches of violence, metal talons clawing at my skull. Tied to the rails of the birthing bed, my mother tugged at the restraints bound tightly around her wrists.

Yearning for someone to be in her corner, this woman who had committed no crime cried out to my father, "I don't think I can take much more of this!"

He looked coolly down upon her sweat-covered face like he was just disturbed from reading his newspaper at the kitchen table and replied, "Well, I guess you'll just have to, won't you?"

Those icy, metal talons eventually yanked me into a world of screams. Simultaneously, the cold, black hole of apathy and indifference towards her devoured my mother's vibrance. The medical staff, with white coats and surgical masks, untying my mother's wrists, were faceless except for their ignorant eyes. With me trembling uncontrollably in her arms, Mom and I both raged against the dying of the light in our eyes. Together, we experienced the extreme cruelty of institutional abuse in the labor and delivery unit of Rochester Memorial Hospital.

What surprised me upon hearing this story from Aunt Jean was learning of the repetitive karma I had gone through, not just once when I was pregnant with my daughter, nor even just twice with what happened ten years later, but actually three times did this karma of restraint abuse happen to me. It started while being one with Mom, as I felt what she was feeling. We were tied down together, while I was in her and emerging from her.

Instead of staff and Dad being behind her and working to calm her while she was hysterical with the agonizing pain of me apparently not wanting to leave the safety of her womb, the routine in those days was to tie women down when they were freaking out during childbirth. Such was the warzone of American life into which I was born. Nothing could change that. Nothing could change the events of my life.

But no one could stop me from changing myself and my karmic destiny, from working to transform my life at a fundamental level from one of horror into a life of safety in the home I would one day discover in my heart. Instead of being dominated by the disrespect and damage done to me, I would then start to see my past as rich with life experiences leading me to become a person of great dignity who could more capably fulfill her immensely meaningful purpose in life.

In childhood, the inextricable bond between Mom and me found me crying inconsolably into my pillow every night when I sensed she was "gone" from me in catatonic depression on a mental ward after her suicide attempt. No one told me, as a fourth-grader, what was going on with her, but I felt it. Now, due to this same inextricable bond, as I transcend the sufferings of birth and death with my spiritual practice and live with an awareness of my debt of gratitude towards her, Mom is happy too. The karma of violence that kept repeating in my family and in my life no longer has the power to control me. The day I walked out of that police station, I was no longer a victim of violence. That day I began my life as a lion.

EPILOGUE

And the battles continue. As any nail that sticks up will tell you, "Watch out for swinging hammers!" Assault and battery, threats, intimidation, and angry tirades have flown at me from every side since I walked out of that police station in 2008. As if life wanted to test me to see just how much of a lion I *really* am. But every one of these situations has created an opportunity for me to stand up for what I feel is right and change the things deep inside me that block me from my greatest potential and happiness.

Since 2008 I've also experienced unimaginable healing from my worst trauma-induced PTSD, the elimination of lifelong depression, and being relieved of the irrepressible urge to compulsively overeat that had plagued me since 1993. So there's much more I want to tell you. I can hardly wait to share with you about my breakthrough transformation that occurred early in 2015, during which the "curse" of breaking ten thousand mirrors was "lifted". That's when I first experienced complete safety in the nurturing home of my light-filled heart. It was then, too, that I began to develop the understanding that

Buddhism is not about guilt, ever.

But giving an account of my experiences since 2008 will require a future writing journey or this book would become much broader in scope and take *much, much, much* longer to revise. Also, with the new direction my life is taking and goals that have yet to come to fruition, it's important to me that my bigger wishes be fulfilled and at least some of my enormous dreams be realized before sharing these years with you. But by recently coming to a place of wholeness, I thought it best this past year to add to and revise parts of this book again based on a much more uplifted, confident and objective perspective than I had for the previous editions.

So my adventures continue, and I'm so grateful to have learned from some of the most adventurous people in history, especially Nichiren Daishonin. His example of challenging the status quo that left people feeling powerless, of creating spiritual reform in the thirteenth century for the sake of the downtrodden common people, has inspired me time and time again. When things have gotten tougher than I could imagine, studying Nichiren's letters and treatises has reminded me of his compassionate tears of amrita (profound appreciation and joy) during his exiles, extreme poverty, severe illness, physical abuse, and barely avoided execution by the Japanese government—*all* of which he triumphed over completely. His victorious life infuses me with the greatest kind of courage to keep moving forward like he always did, and to galvanize a similarly altruistic spirit to keep working in service and support of others' happiness to the best of my ability. This actually deepens my sense of appreciation for difficulties. That way, just like it takes air resistance for a plane to gain altitude, I can see obstacles as opportunities to become more uplifted, courageous, and compassionate, as well as stronger and wiser, so that I can encourage myself and others better.

So now when negativity comes my way, the important thing for me remains: what is my behavior in all this? Though I'd like to think of myself as perfectly graceful in all my human interactions, it just ain't necessarily so.

Nichiren once wrote: "What does Bodhisattva Never Disparaging's profound respect for people signify? The real purpose of the appearance in this world of Shakyamuni Buddha...lies in his behavior as a human being."[16]

As much as I've wished to be in charge of my behavior through the years, the thoughts and feelings governing my actions have sometimes been counterintuitive to the best interests of those involved, including myself. A whacky neurophysiology tends to do this. So, did I find the solution I sought to help me with this? Was there an Rx solution? The short answer is: Yes! (But not just one solution.)

The long answer is: I couldn't have finished this book for the 2012 memoir contest without using a mineral supplement that helped me stay focused and out of the "grandiose psychosis zone." But I also couldn't have finished several years of revisions without the assistance of psychiatric medications.

As for what I consider an over-the-counter Rx solution, this mineral supplement I'm refer-ring to was the only thing I used from late 2009 to mid-2012. Regarding this mineral, in the state of Texas are towns whose water supply contains trace amounts of natural lithium. Studies have shown that those particular towns have lower average crime rates and fewer problems with mental illness.

I found out through a friend in the Asheville Radical Mental Health Collective (ARMHC, a local Icarus Project initiative) that a mineral supplement named Lithium Orotate works to alleviate major symptoms of bipolar disorder for some people. In his case, use of Lithium Orotate stopped the effects of the pharmaceutical drug Lithium Carbonate that had decreased his kidney function to 25%, and he was able to increase his kidney function to 75% while using Lithium Orotate.

Although orotate has helped some people with bipolar and has been used by the general public for better focus and concentration, Lithium Orotate hasn't helped everyone I know with bipolar who's tried it. For those like me that have found it helpful, it's not a cure-all. But for over two years I found the tiny amount of lithium contained in Lithium Orotate to be all I needed to keep hyper-mania at bay.

As for why it works differently than Lithium Carbonate, some research indicates that this form of lithium crosses the blood-brain barrier in a way that the carbonate form cannot. Because of that a much smaller amount of lithium is required. Other research contradicts the blood-brain barrier theory.

But all that mattered to me was that it didn't require a saturation of my body chemistry with hundreds and hundreds of milligrams of lithium the way the medication Lithium Carbonate did, so I didn't lose my imagination and creativity. I could sleep better, and I didn't end up numb and lifeless. Many of my symptoms got eliminated, and I maintained my geyser of gratitude in the process.

I'd like to add that some people have used the medication Lithium Carbonate with seemingly little or no problem. If you are thinking about trying Lithium Orotate, *please consult your doctor first, and be aware that different brands and formulas of this mineral supplement can have varying effects.*[17] (It would be awesome if studies were started again comparing Orotate to Carbonate, including a reasonable adjustment for the dramatic difference in amounts required for the desired effects so as to have a substantive understanding about the different effects they have on people.)

And as it turns out, a year or so before my friend in the ARMHC told me about it, my psychiatric nurse practitioner had actually recommended that I try Lithium Orotate. But I had thought she was referring to Lithium Carbonate. Neither of us ever realized the confusion until much later, after I told her I'd started using it.

After such success with Lithium Orotate for two and a half years, in the summer of 2012 extreme stressors prompted me to take psychiatric medication again. I've tried a couple different ones which have helped in certain ways.

Returning to Geodon eliminated any fear I had of grandiosity, psychosis or sleeplessness returning. It also got rid of the anxiety I had then that was so extreme that to touch my abdomen anywhere from the base of my neck to my hips was intensely painful. The intensity of that anxiety and pain also made my emotions volatile during stressful times. But after Geodon made the anxiety go away, numbness set in, as did nearly unrelenting depression.

Then Lamictal, an anti-convulsant, entered the picture a couple years later. Adding it and lessening the Geodon lessened the frequency of my crying jags, but heavy depression remained. Outwardly I could be cheerful, optimistic and bright at times due to my practice. But I couldn't feel the light in my heart until the lifting of "the curse." Since that lifting I've been able to develop a strong, consistent and more correct practice, which makes the ups and downs of life enjoyable in ways I didn't imagine they could be.

As for my imagination, that has been greatly enlivened since the uplift too. I used to blame the medications for how bad I felt. Now I see that although they do have drawbacks, the tradeoffs are worth it for the time being. Most importantly I can sleep rather than stay up for days that has always taken me to that highly dangerous place. So until I heal from trauma and dysfunction fully enough I will consider Rx solutions necessary. I'm actually grateful to have them as part of my kit for an optimum quality of life.

Still, some of their effects bother me a lot. Although I greatly enjoy hiking and being by the creek, my feeling of connection with Nature and Earth and my sense of awe and wonder that human beings are hard-wired to experience are very inhibited. And while I still have a passion for writing poetry and music, it doesn't flow readily anymore. But with this combination of drugs, although I still feel people's physical and emotional pain in my body and heart/mind (which I believe happens to me due to what research has identified as a higher than normal supply of mirror neurons in the brain which dramatically increases my sensitivity to the environment and to how other people feel) I'm not easily swayed by it. And the wonderful thing about my drug use is that it can't take away the tears of joyous gratitude and inspiration I enjoy from my spiritual practice, my underlying happiness, my sense of humor, nor my excitement about life and the future.

Even though depression has departed, I still feel heaviness in my heart at times, but I've overcome the fear that chronic, debilitating depresssion is returning. I know it can't entrap me anymore. Rather, these experiences occur due to situations that are happening in my life. Fortunately, I can always take value-creating actions right away, chant, and do my human revolution to change me, my relationships and circumstances. And this lightens my heart back up again.

My karmic destiny changes for the better every time I make good decisions and create positive value instead of suffering for myself or others, so I'm very thankful for all of the Rx solutions that have helped me deal with life along the way, both the over-the-counter and pharmaceutical solutions.

Working on this memoir has been a challenging yet very healing endeavor. It's something I recommend everybody try. Sharing one's secrets not only helps free oneself but can also help others. And because of chanting, I've changed the misfortune I've shared about in this book into fortune. The events of my past have all turned into gems adorning the treasure tower that is my life.

One additional secret I'd like to divulge is that for many years I was so terrified by the experiences in my mind in my childhood bedroom that it felt like my spirit was constantly trying to escape my body through my head. But thanks to the encouragement of my Panamanian Teddy Bear friend, I changed my desperation to be free of this suffering into determination. Soon, one very strong chanting session stopped my spirit from wanting to flee. My therapist at the time even commented that I was no longer brittle with rage.

Life has taken such turns that I have even been able to enjoy the depths of loving physical intimacy with a man, and I'm thankful I've chanted for Rocky.

Another healing opportunity has been my volunteer work as a presenter for the In Our Own Voice (IOOV) interactive program[18] organized by the National Alliance on Mental Illness (NAMI). Through this work I've met a number of people who have found their own paths to recovery and are living contributive lives.

The Icarus Project I referred to earlier sees mental health challenges as dangerous gifts to be cultivated and taken care of rather than as a disease or disorder needing to be "cured" or "overcome." Like certain ethnicities, Icarus is against the pharmaceutical companies' push to medicate everyone. I agree that this is not the ultimate solution by any means.

But however one interprets these altered

states of consciousness, the hope is to see the energy of physical and psychological healing engaged in by people everywhere, including myself, move us towards a more peaceful world. A peace that overtakes the energy of war's devastation, including the violence in war that took my grandfather's eye and came home to roost as either PTSD or bipolar disorder in the rearing of his children with his fist. I say either PTSD or bipolar because one can look like the other. In Grampa's case, he was never diagnosed, and even though he had intense emotional volatility, he remained functional all his life with no medical intervention. So either/or. We don't know.

And this makes me wonder whether it's been genes or PTSD that has been passed down through the generations of my family, manifesting as what looks like bipolar. After all, my mother, one aunt who says she started having symptoms of bipolar late in life, and I all experienced violence in childhood, mine starting at birth. Maybe that's when and why my bio-energetic-chemistry started to go haywire. I'll only know for sure when I heal from PTSD enough.

As for IOOV, along with helping those who do these interactive presentations, this program educates students from middle school age through to the university level, as well as trauma survivors, social service workers, police officers, psychiatric inpatients, medical providers, church congregations and many other groups with the real life stories of people recovering from severe neurobiological disorders. IOOV places great importance on facilitating discussion amongst audience members throughout its presentations, so more and more people are talking openly about this topic. For me, what could be more encouraging and freeing? IOOV helped me come out of the closet about my bipolar label. I'm not ashamed anymore. A program like In Our Own Voice can help you or someone you love too.

And who knows? It may turn out, as I continue along my healing journey, that my bio-energetic-chemistry may change enough to need no more chemical intervention. Or I may find that psychosis is part and parcel of my particular experience in today's stressful society. Is it simply the spirit's imagination gone wild in connection with a trauma-induced energetic imbalance that could be "tamed" and balanced naturally and holistically in time? Will I turn out to be like people with diabetes who no matter what behavioral changes they make must still take medication to control it? Or one day be like diabetics who through simple diet and exercise modifications have healed from their condition and have gotten off of insulin and oral medication completely? One person in the ARMHC overcame his psychosis and other life-inhibiting symptoms through a strict diet and staying away from the public for a couple years. I've read about other people getting well mentally and emotionally who have left medication behind. This indicates that anything is possible.

Maybe it'll turn out that I just need therapeutic modalities that I haven't tried or discovered yet to replace prescription Rx solutions. Mega-doses of vitamins have helped some people with schizophrenia. Infra-red waves made a huge difference in the life of someone I know who used to have panic attacks and extreme anxiety constantly. Someone receiving regular acupuncture treatments who was able to develop excellent sleep hygiene found medication no longer necessary for her bipolar except in rare instances when her sleep regimen faltered.

Massage therapy is helping me with physical pain and now includes releasing emotions trapped in the tissues. Because of this therapy and what it's taught me about my own ability to do healing body work with nurturing-touch, I've been able to increase my capacity to assist in others' healing processes to significantly reduce or eliminate stubborn, chronic, intense pain.

Other things that have helped improve my mental & emotional states have been classes in Dialectical Behavioral Therapy (DBT) with coping skills based on mindfulness, Internal Family Systems (IFS) parts work, Eye Movement Desensitization and Reprocessing (EMDR), and binaural beats.

Now Somatic Experiencing (SE) looks promising as a potent psychobiological method for resolving trauma symptoms and relieving chronic stress. I look forward to experimenting with this and other modalities to move me towards ever greater healing and equilibrium. Should they prove necessary, there are also many more healing practices out there for me to research and experiment with. And then there are those humanity hasn't even thought of yet.

I must admit, it would be great to leave medication behind. After all, without more research we don't know the long-term effects of all these psych drugs on the human body. And we already know that some medications cause debilitating health effects even in the short term, like psychiatric medication-related diabetes and unrelenting Parkinson's-like tremors. Lamictal itself can cause death if one is allergic to it. (Fortunately for this increasingly popular drug, a severe rash will usually develop to indicate the allergy before it becomes life-threatening.) Hopefully more personal research and a good bit more healing from PTSD will replace my current need to ingest man-made medication to ensure my optimum quality of life. That's my *ideal* solution anyway.

During In Our Own Voice interactive presentations, after we discuss with an audience our dark days, our process of acceptance, treatments, coping skills and, finally, our successes, hopes and dreams, I love to share one of my favorite quotes from Professor Ikeda. He once wrote:

"There is a saying, 'A small heart gets used to misery and becomes docile, while a great heart towers above misfortune.' True happiness is not the absence of suffering; you cannot have day after day of clear skies. True happiness lies in building a self that stands dignified and indomitable like a great palace—on all days, even when it is raining, snowing or stormy."[19]

So whether or not that *ideal* solution manifests, I'm determined to live a life of undefeatable happiness and achieve my greatest potential, youthfulness and gratitude in the midst of my struggles with bipolar and medication, thanks to my Buddhist practice with the SGI, my wonderfully supportive friends, my recovery and healing work, and the tools I use for wellness, *with* an Rx solution in the mix.

The Veterans Administration made a decision a few years ago to hire thousands more mental health therapists to help soldiers and veterans with PTSD and a host of other psychiatric illnesses. Hopefully this is a sign that more of our society will treat people with psychiatric conditions, including those who are homeless or imprisoned, with greater dignity and kindness—for those coming back from war and for all those suffering from a war within their own minds and hearts.

On that note, a couple years ago I decided to protect my rights as a potential patient in a locked psychiatric facility by creating my own notarized Psychiatric Advance Directive (PAD) to indicate just exactly what treatment I will allow. An acquaintance of mine who has long worked in the mental health field was just a couple years ago forced to take the debilitating anti-psychotic drug Haldol in a local hospital even though he'd told them beforehand that it was harmful to him. So my PAD outlines what medications work to help or potentially harm me.

Most important to me is that my directive also states that, if physical restraints were absolutely necessary to protect me from hurting others or myself, that *only* a straightjacket is allowed, *not* four-point restraints. Although a 2008 investigative report to the United Nations Human Rights Council defined the prolonged use of four-point restraints as torture, it's not against the law yet and is still an all too common practice today. In just the past year, a friend's young son was tied down for a long time in a North Carolina state psychiatric facility. As his Legal Guardian she was supposed to have been consulted during this incident, but she was not informed of what was done to him until sometime after his "treatment" was administered.

I dearly hope this book will help engender justice about this. There is such a need for strict regulations regarding restraint use in psych facilities across the nation, much like there are laws strictly regulating this in nursing homes for the elderly with Alzheimer's and dementia. After all, it creates scars that are very difficult to heal. And the worst thing is that, although its not common, young people have died in four-point restraints.

As for PAD's, NAMI North Carolina is working on this issue. NAMI NC lobbyists aim to move our North Carolina legislators to create a law so that they become legally-binding documents here like they are in some other states. What's crucial is better public awareness.

But the way things are, it's no wonder I'm protecting my rights and denoting my preference for a straightjacket. Such a device enables the patient to keep their arms crossed in front of them, which I imagine would feel protective, like being forced into the position of a self-hug rather than one's abdomen being exposed and vulnerable in four-point. Though I'm sure a straightjacket is no fun, the idea of that self-hug feels very reassuring somehow. But, of course, one hopes such extreme precautions would never become necessary.

Here I'd like to point out that I have been blessed with some wonderful therapists, psychologists and psychiatrists over the years (like Amanda, Peter, Pierre and Ed.) There are many out there, as well as numerous inpatient facilities and outpatient mental health centers providing good care with great kindness. But you never know how life will unfold, and I can't stress too strongly how much the act of creating a PAD and getting it notarized has helped me feel more secure and empowered regarding my future treatment in the mental health system. That, and having friends who are ready to stand by me to help enforce these directives should that become necessary. I wish such protections for all those potentially in need of psychiatric services.

And we could learn a lot from techniques utilized in some mental health facilities in other countries. Their approach towards the suffering individual includes policies to treat the whole person and their family relationships holistically. Through their forward-thinking therapeutic practices, use of restraints is prohibited, and many individuals recover completely and return to living normal lives without drugs ever being administered.

Having been a nail that got pounded down so many times, coming to a place of self-worth to stand up for my rights as a human being and then speak out for others took me many years to actualize. But it was worth it to get to this place because putting one's passion to work alongside others for a cause, like for peace, the environment, human rights, or some other endeavor to make a positive difference adds hope to the world even as it adds to one's own self-esteem. It's great to be empowered to transform the binds of karma that trapped me in suffering into a mission to create boundless value in the world. No longer burdened by the feeling that I'm the world's unluckiest soul, at times I feel like the *most fortunate* being in the whole universe.

Again, from Dr. Ikeda, "No one can better bask in summer's balm than those who have endured winter's bite. Similarly, it is those who have suffered through life's darkest hours who are able to truly savor the bright dawn of happiness. The person who has transformed the worst of fate into the best of fortune is life's champion."[20]

My continuing human revolution and the transformations I've witnessed in countless other people convinces me that, like Mrs. Roosevelt said, if we as a people believe in something with all our hearts and work for it, we can make the impossible possible, even peace on a global scale. I mean, one person experiencing peace, empowerment, spiritual transformation and deep happiness encouraging someone else creates world peace, one person, one relationship at a time—in direct opposition to the violent times we live in. And no matter what "dog whistle frequency" you respond to—what spiritual/religious path calls to you—through local interfaith dialogues in cities and towns across the globe we are building peace among us every single day. It just doesn't make news headlines.

And personally, what I'd never imagined some twenty years ago during my most horrific hospitalization, is that I am utilizing the energy of compassion and justice that I once believed was a nuclear bomb in my chest to support efforts towards the abolition of nuclear weapons.

Of course, with Fukushima, the world not long ago witnessed the dangerous and harmful use of nuclear power. But nuclear weapons issues aren't in the forefront of people's minds except in cases where countries unfriendly to the west might use them. (Or a presidential candidate says he's against nuclear proliferation but then insanely implies that Japan, South Korea and Saudi Arabia should have nuclear weapons.)

But our media doesn't discuss the approximately 7,000 nuclear warheads the U.S. has and the 7,300 that Russia has. That these could annihilate humankind hundreds of times over isn't a sensational topic for them to cover since proliferation in our country has been continuing for many decades. A lot of young people aren't even aware that such a threat exists.

However, just a few years ago thousands of representatives of faith-based groups from all over the world came together in Melbourne, Australia for a nuclear abolition exhibition and conference hosted by the SGI. In addition, many non-profit groups are working towards this aim, while college students and other youth of SGI are determined through one-to-one dialogues and public gatherings to galvanize enough support to achieve world-wide nuclear weapons abolition by 2030. And the youth of the SGI don't make commitments lightly. All this spells great hope— for a foundation of security for all future generations. Witness hope: "Revolution In You" at https://www.youtube.com/watch?v=1KQ-fc9ltjE

As for Mom and Dad? Chanting for Dad's happiness has enabled me to develop appreciation for him. I think if it wasn't for his promise to help repay my college loans, the stress of that looming financial burden would have seriously interfered with my ability to finish my degree. Thanks to Dad's personal tutoring, I finished one very difficult computer class for my degree too. That's actually one of my favorite memories of the two of us together. Fortunately for him, for over ten years now Dad's been married to a wonderful woman. My third stepmother lives according to spiritual principles and has a terrifically supportive attitude towards me. For that, I am very thankful.

French actress Sarah Bernhardt was

quoted as saying, "Life begets life. Energy creates energy. It is by spending oneself that one becomes rich."[21] I love it that Dad has chosen to spend his golden years volunteering his expertise with computers in service of others. A man of few words, I imagine he's proud of his "wordy," award-winning daughter. (The contest may have only been county-wide, but the many entries from gifted writers in this area made it a challenging competition. Secretly dreaming of authoring my life story in a compelling way during those years I slept under that white, knobby bedspread, I never realized what it would take to have a compelling life story though!) And if he thinks about it, Dad's probably more relieved than I am that I haven't seen the inside of a psych ward, except as a visitor, in over a decade.

Mom once told me about something that happened during her pregnancy with me. She used a suppository for some pain she had "down there." It melted purple on the way out. Since her recovery from sadness, I asked if she'd thought when carrying me how purple was a symbol of royalty, and did she ever think of me as such a royal child, like a real princess or something? I felt very shy in asking her this.

But (of course), she replied, "Yes. I did."

In 2012 the protective functions in the universe saw fit to provide me the means to visit Mom after being unable to do so for five years, my chance to treat her like a queen in every way. What a world of good it did me to see her so happy!

Going with Mom to my first Twelve-Step meeting when I visited her for a couple of my teenage summers, I've learned since then that some people with addictions of one sort or another experience some symptoms of bipolar disorder while they are active in their addiction. But *sometimes*, when folks develop a life based on spiritual principles, these symptoms diminish or disappear altogether. That's how I had wished it would be for me. All my life, I didn't want to accept that I had bipolar disorder. Maybe one day I'll make the impossible possible and find that enough healing from all my PTSD will eliminate the underlying causes of my bipolar experiences.

But as for now, I don't have that awful longing anymore. I wouldn't be who I am— someone with great empathy for the sufferings of others who imparts hope—the creative bipolar daughter of a gentle, creative, bipolar mother, a mother who readily sees to the heart of things and reads people well. (She's written some ingenious poetry and prose herself.) A mom who imprinted her giant heart on me with great big, squeezable bear hugs, complete with yummy noises like she was eating me up, during our few early years together, as if to make sure I'd never forget how her love felt.

With appreciation for all the women and mothers who have encouraged me, and especially in Mom's honor, I'd like to share the following poem, hoping she and I will one day meet her granddaughter, Jeruleve.....

When I was two/I cannot help me loving you

You're so big! I'm so small.
Your life glows and towers tall!
I love it when you pick up me
and sit me on your loving knee
The prickles from your thighs' shaved hairs
They tickle-prick my legs when bare
But would I dare to say a word
In protest, NO! I'll hug your girth
and let you with your arms so wide
encompass me from every side
I'll wiggle like a wriggly worm
I'll poke you lightly, make you squirm
I'll hear your chesty laughter loud
I'll giggle and I'll kiss you proud
Your lips upon my belly buzz
Makes me shriek; it really does
I cannot help me loving you
My mother-friend; all trusted, true.

Acknowledgments and Offerings of Gratitude

First and foremost, I'd like to thank my most essential teacher, *Nam-myoho-renge-kyo,* which is my life itself. Of course, I also offer boundless gratitude to my supremely heroic teacher, Nichiren Daishonin, for boldly declaring and sharing this Buddhism despite horrific persecution. Nichiren Buddhism can empower anyone to bring forth the courage, hope, compassion, creative wisdom and strong life force necessary to overcome all the problems and sufferings that are part of life to realize the greatest kind of happiness, founded on supremely enjoyable gratitude. And one doesn't have to throw away all the beliefs they've grown up with.

If you'd like to know more about this Buddhist practice and the philosophy behind it or to find an SGI meeting near you, please visit www.sgi.org for a wealth of free information. SGI meetings are always free and open to everyone.

I also offer my deepest appreciation to my most esteemed mentor, SGI President Daisaku Ikeda, and his profoundly supportive wife Kaneko. Dr. Ikeda's many decades of tireless actions as a grateful disciple have taught me the meaning of winning in life and the path to becoming a winner. Thank you, Sensei, for believing in me more than I could possibly have believed in myself for so long.

I am also, of course, deeply indebted to the first president of the Soka Gakkai, Tsunesaburo Makiguchi, who gave his life to protect the true spirit of Nichiren Daishonin's Buddhism, and his successor, second Soka Gakkai President, Josei Toda, who carried on that spirit. I am also thankful to their wives and mothers, the women who selflessly nurtured and supported them.

Certainly I'm forever indebted to my parents, Carol and Glenn, for giving me life and for wanting to have me. I'm so deeply grateful to Jeruleve, too, for the gift of the experience of giving birth to her. I am also thankful to Brian and my extended family, especially Grandpa and Grandma Schirmer, Grandpa and Grandma Richards, Grandpa and Grandma Long, Uncle Stan, Aunt Glenda, Aunt Jean, Uncle Jerry, Aunt Wanda, Uncle Dean, Aunt Doris, Cliff, Curt, Colleen and Cynthia. And there's my debt of gratitude to all people who, in one incarnation or another, have been my parents.

I wish to also mention my gratitude to all living beings, and to Earth and Nature, for all their gifts which sustain all of our lives. I only hope we'll learn to better repay our debts of gratitude to them.

I want to whole-heartedly thank Nichiren's pure-hearted disciples since the 13th century and the members of SGI around the world, especially the pioneers. I've received support and encouragement from as far away as Japan. Specifically, I'd like to thank Kazumi, Terry, Mei, Ikuyo, Yaeko, Kumi, David, John, Kimiko, Akiko, Akemi, Joe, Mary Margaret, TJ, Fernando, Karen, Devrick, Kathy, Danny, Stephanie, Ann, Olabisi, Sharon, Laura Lee, Rebecca, Roger, Deneen, Terri, Joanne, Jo, Gail, Maria, Anna, Barnaby, Mariko, David, Beverley, Brickey and Jeff. I'd also like to thank Joan, Ross, Debra Sue, Sarah, Jenny, Liliana, and confidants Barbara, Robyn, Gabi, Margie, Amanda, Steve, and Cecelia, along with Rebecca H., who always has my back in an emergency, as well as the many wonderful members of my recovery community and many other dear friends who have cared about me along the way.

Starting with Kayuni, many women in the SGI and recovery have lovingly helped me do my human revolution and heal a lot of my maternal issues as spiritual sisters and aunts of the best kind. Many spiritual uncles and brothers I've known have done the same for me with my paternal issues. So many people have been protective forces for me, and I'm determined to pay this forward for the rest of my life.

I wish to offer a special thanks to Mary Anne, the woman who believed in my writing to such a degree that I was able to jump confidently into the memoir contest waters. I also wish to thank the Friends of the Black Mountain Library who held the memoir contest, the Buncombe County library system, Nancy, the seminar instructor, and Denise, the final judge of the contest who became my biggest fan. I would like to also thank my patient editor, Elizabeth Clontz, for her dedicated and exhaustive work on the first edition, as well as all the other friends and acquaintances who have given me constructive criticism on the book—including but not limited to David, Karen, Cynthia, Tracy, Melissa, Yvonne, Debra Sue and Jessica—and finally, Salem Rana and Pam Mortimer for their technical expertise throughout the publication process.

Thank you, all, *so very much.*

References

1. Roosevelt, Eleanor. *Tomorrow is Now* (Harper & Row, 1963), p 4 & 128.

2. *The Lotus Sutra*, original translation from Sanskrit into Chinese by Kumarajiva, translated into English by Burton Watson (Columbia University Press, 1993)

3. Bodhisattva: This is a Sanskrit term for a being who aspires to attain Buddhahood and carries out altruistic practices to achieve that goal. Compassion predominates in bodhisattvas, who postpone their own entry into nirvana in order to lead others toward enlightenment. It is said that the bodhisattva spirit shines in those who aspire to impart joy and remove the sufferings of others.

4. *Inside the Nichiren Shoshu Priesthood, How the Priesthood failed to destroy the SGI* (The Association of Youthful Priests for the Reformation of Nichiren Shoshu, 2010) p 19.

5. Chanting *Nam-myoho-renge-kyo* is essentially a declaration of the enlightened nature in all life, a vow to manifest it in oneself and others. It is not praise to an external deity but rather the means to manifest Buddhahood, the highest state of life present within all people, a state of fearless wisdom and happiness free of delusion and also deep compassion; understanding the connection between all life, a Buddha faces the sufferings of all beings and derives joy from teaching others how to awaken to the wondrous potential within.

The Lotus Sutra is regarded by Nichiren Buddhists as the most profound teaching of Buddhism. Nichiren declared that the full title (in Sanskrit, *Saddharma-pundarika-sutra*, translated as *Myoho-renge-kyo*) contains the essence of the sutra itself. Though Nam-myoho-renge-kyo is meant to be understood as a whole, it can also be viewed word by word. Each syllable contains multiple meanings, but the most basic translation is as follows:

--*myo (sad)*: mystic, wonderful, [unfathomable]. This represents the wondrous nature of enlightenment.

--*ho (dharma)*: Law, or phenomena. Often *myo* and *ho* are combined as *myoho*, or Mystic Law, meaning the essential truth of Buddhism, [the universal law or principle underlying all phenomena].

--*renge (pundarika)*: Lotus blossom. [Since the lotus flower blooms and seeds simultaneously], this represents the universality of cause and effect. Additionally, a lotus blooms in muddy water [but is never sullied by it], and so a lotus is symbolic of the inherent Buddhahood in all life, no matter how troubled or deluded that life may be.

--*kyo (sutra)*: Nichiren defined *kyo* as the voice of all living beings, and the eternal truth of Buddhism.

To these characters, Nichiren added *nam*, derived from the Sanskrit word *namas*, meaning devotion, dedication, [to fuse with or unite with].

Through chanting, Nichiren Buddhists awaken their enlightened potential, and from this state, examine the various challenges and benefits in their lives and generate the wisdom to proceed with joy, no matter how great the struggle before them.

(Source: Ikeda, Daisaku. *Buddhism Day by Day-- Wisdom for Modern Life* (Middle Way Press, 2006) p 7, 8 & 9.—by the editorial committee)

6. Baker Acted: To be involuntarily committed to a mental health treatment facility.

7. Daishonin, Nichiren. *The Writings of Nichiren Daishonin* (Soka Gakkai, 1999) p 1137.

8. IBID p 851.

9. Nichiren Daishonin identifies three kinds of treasures that humans hold dear—

Treasures of the storehouse: financial and material success

Treasures of the body: vibrant health and well-being

Treasures of the heart (the most valuable of all) include: sincerity, gratitude, honesty, integrity, perseverance, courage, compassion, the spirit to fight for truth, justice and the happiness of all people, kindness, generosity, altruism, wisdom, hope, profound appreciation and joy, expanding consciousness, inner light, a sense of the inter-connectedness of all life, confidence, humility and supreme dignity.

10. Ikeda, Daisaku. *The New Human Revolution*, (SGI-USA, 1995) vol. 1, p iv.

11. Second Soka Gakkai [Value-Creating Society] president Josei Toda used the term *human revolution* to describe the process of attaining Buddhahood, a self-transformation achieved through Nichiren Buddhist practice within the Soka Gakkai International. This transformation involves breaking the shackles of our ego-centered 'lesser selves' and revealing our 'greater selves', wherein we experience deep compassion and joyfully take action for the sake of others, and ultimately, all humanity.

(Source: *Living Buddhism* (SGI-USA, April 2013), p 3.)

12. Kosen-rufu: Literally, "to widely declare and spread". Kosen-rufu refers to the process of securing lasting peace and happiness for all humankind by establishing the humanistic ideals of Nichiren Buddhism in society based on profound reverence for life.

13. Ikeda, Daisaku. *Learning from the Gosho: The Eternal Teachings of Nichiren Daishonin* (SGI-USA, 1997) p 44.

14. Mohandas K. (a.k.a. Mahatma) Gandhi, Martin Luther King, Jr. and Daisaku Ikeda, three men from three different cultures and continents, have followed a common path of profound dedication and achievement in improving the lives of all people. "Gandhi, King, Ikeda: A Legacy of Building Peace" conveys the themes and pivotal principles in the lives of these giants of the 20th century. This traveling exhibit, commissioned by Dr. Lawrence Carter, Baptist minister and dean of the Martin Luther King Jr. International Chapel at Morehouse College in Atlanta, opened in 2001. A community builder's prize is awarded each year to individuals who epitomize the principles demonstrated in the lives of these three great champions of peace and human rights. For more information, please visit: http://www.morehouse.edu/mlkchapel/peace_ex hibit/index.html

15. The *World Tribune* is published by the SGI-USA three times a month, along with a monthly study journal, *Living Buddhism.*

16. Daishonin, Nichiren. *The Writings of Nichiren Daishonin* (Soka Gakkai, 1999) p 852.
17. The difference between the amounts of the supplement lithium orotate that works best for each individual can vary considerably.
18. In Our Own Voice: https://www.nami.org/Find-Support/NAMI-Programs/NAMI-In-Our-Own-Voice
19. Ikeda, Daisaku. *Learning from the Gosho: The Eternal Teachings of Nichiren Daishonin* (SGI-USA, 1997) p 241.
20. Ikeda, Daisaku. *Buddhism Day by Day-- Wisdom for Modern Life* (Middle Way Press, 2006) p 222.
21. *Quotable Women* (Running Press, 1989).

About the Author

Kitty Richards is the first-prize winner of the Friends of the Black Mountain Library 2012 memoir contest, which received entries from throughout the Buncombe County library system. She continues to write and work for peace. The Icarus Project, NAMI, and the Depression and Bipolar Support Alliance (DBSA), are some national organizations with local support groups throughout the U.S. To learn more about the Buddhist humanism referred to in this memoir please visit www.sgi.org. SGI meetings are always free and open to everyone.

65782702R00170

Made in the USA
Lexington, KY
24 July 2017